WINSTER

A PEAK DISTRICT VILLAGE REMEMBERS

Winster Local History Group
2000

Times have changed

When you come to think about it, as time goes on and you've gone through all this - same as I say, no water in the house, no flush toilet, no electricity, no telephone - how would some of them really go on today, I wonder? How many people would walk it right from Middleton to Mill Close Mine and do all them hours - a forty-eight-hour week - and when they'd done the work they had all that way to walk back? It didn't matter whether it rained, snowed or what - they still had to go. They still went through the snow and went through the rain and worked like that, and had to go back to it for a little wage, day in and day out. Yet today people get all that given - not worked for it - they've had it give 'em, and they're still not satisfied.
[Bert Boam]

WINSTER

A PEAK DISTRICT VILLAGE REMEMBERS

Winster Local History Group
2000

© 2000 Winster Local History Group

First published June 2000

Reprinted 2005 by

Winster Local History Group
c/o The Post Office
Main Street
Winster
Matlock DE4 2DH
Tel: (01629) 650034

Village Web Site: www.winster.org

ISBN: 1 901522 83 0

Produced by
Landmark Publishing Ltd,
Ashbourne Hall, Cokayne Avenue
Ashbourne, Derbyshire
DE6 1EJ England
Tel: (01335) 347349 Fax: (01335) 347303
e-mail: landmark@clara.net
Web Site: www.landmarkpublishing.co.uk

British Library Cataloguing in Publication Data: a catalogue record for this
book is available from the British Library.

Print: Cromwell Press Ltd., Trowbridge, Wiltshire

Designed by: James Allsopp

Front cover: Winster painted by Bill Kirby
Page 3: Shothouse Spout, c. 1934, with Eric Roper (in cap)
collecting water in churns.

CONTENTS

West Bank, Winster.

West Bank. The building in the centre is now demolished.

Winster is an ancient lead-mining village in the Derbyshire Peak District. It existed at the time of the Domesday Book (1086), and grew into a modest market community, until a boom in lead mining in the seventeenth and eighteenth centuries turned the village into a prosperous small town. Flooding in the mines became a problem as the workings got deeper, and eventually it forced many of them to close. The last working mine at Mill Close, two miles north-east of Winster, employed large numbers of local men until it closed in 1938. A number of the buildings on the imposing Main Street, some of which were once shops, date from the hey-day of mining. The two grandest buildings are Winster Market House (now owned by the National Trust) and Winster Hall. The cottages which huddle together on the hillside, known as Winster Bank, are more likely to have been the modest homes of the poorer miners, quarrymen and agricultural workers and their families. They spread out between two steep roads, East Bank and West Bank, and are linked by a web of narrow pathways. All around are mineshafts and grassy mounds left over from the period of lead mining. In the 1950s an estate of council houses was built at Leacroft, on the eastern approaches.

In contrast to past times, few of the residents now work in the village, and this fact, together with the rise of motor transport, has brought the demise of much of the old community. But although there has been change there has not been decline, for Winster is one of the most lively villages in the area, with a school, shops, a garage, two pubs, a church, two chapels, playing fields, a medical centre, a newly refurbished village hall, and many flourishing activity groups. Much of this liveliness can be experienced during Winster Wakes, especially on Wakes Saturday, which is usually the first in July.

Carnival procession along Main Street on Wakes Saturday 1982.
The building in the background is the Market House.

The feeling that the old village life was slipping away was one of the motives that lay behind the formation in 1996 of the Local History Group. Its declared aim is 'to promote awareness and understanding of Winster's history through research, publication, talks and exhibitions'. We hoped from the start that the History Group's activities would help foster a spirit of togetherness and inter-est in the village, and we like to think that this has proved to be the case, with membership at one time reaching sixty (from an adult population of about six hundred). Our activities are of two sorts: monthly talks throughout the winter on subjects of local interest, and informal workshop groups that meet through-out the year in people's homes. The workshops have concentrated on such things as assembling an archive of photographs and documents, investigating individual buildings, working on material for a village map, and recording the memories of residents and former residents. This last enterprise, which we call our Oral History Project, now comes to fruition with the publication of this book.

We first began making our recordings in February 1997. Initially people were rather uncertain about what we were doing, especially as those asking the questions were mainly newcomers to Winster. But now that the project has come to be better understood we find we have no shortage of volunteers. There are many we have not yet interviewed. Nor are we only interested in times long past, because we recognise that history does not stand still. So our archive of tapes, which now numbers about fifty, will continue to expand, we hope, in years to come.

In preparing the transcripts of the tapes for publication we have had to make changes, such as removing the words of the interviewers, taking out repeated material, and grouping the transcribed texts according to subject matter. There have been difficult decisions to make, such as the extent to which we should standardise and 'correct' the language. We knew that if we went too far in that direction we might lose the naturalness of the spoken words, so on the whole we have tried to keep changes to a minimum. Mostly it has just been a matter of clarification. Another consideration was the local dialect. One of our infor-mants, Stan Heathcote, is so distinctive in his use of local speech that we have retained it (with his permission) in our transcriptions, so far as the limits of the ordinary alphabet allow! In short, we have tried to follow a common-sense approach and treat every problem individually. But it has not been all problems. It has been a pleasure for us to meet people and to enjoy their stories of past times. What they have told us is full of interest, and we have found that many people are natural storytellers. Readers will judge this for themselves.

The material in this book has two main features: it is personal and it is re-membered. Because it is personal, we have only included it with the express permission of those concerned. And because it is remembered it needs to be distinguished from factual history. Sequences of events easily become distorted as people reach back into their memories, and dates tend to get disregarded altogether. So this is not a history book. Therefore we have not checked and changed what people have told us, beyond putting right obvious inaccuracies and contradictions. We have, though, tried to remove anything that might be taken amiss – but not to the extent of making the subject matter bland and uninteresting. But we are realistic enough to know that it is virtually impossible

Winster Wisdom: 'You canna take a stocking off a bare leg.'

not to offend someone, however careful we are, either by what we have included or by what we have left out. We can only ask readers to bear in mind that our intention all along has been to help Winster people understand and be proud of their distinctive local heritage, and to give the wider public some idea of what life was like in a rural community during the course of the last century.

The membership of the Oral History Project has fluctuated over the three years since we began. The following people are or have been members: Barbara Berry, Hilary Campbell, Betty Dawes, Gill Elliott, Freda Forster, Frances Hope, Geraldine Hopkinson, Geoff Lester, Sue Mills, Christine Renouf, Simon Reynolds, Jan Shiers and Hilary Tomlinson. We are grateful for having received valuable help in one form or another from Helen Bastin, Carolyn Brook, Joe Kewin, Marg Lester, John Mills, Brenda Newsam, Rod Shiers, Rosie Strauss and Mair Walters. And, of course, we warmly thank all those who agreed to be interviewed, without whom this project could never even have been begun.

Preparing this book has been a shared responsibility, but three people have had a greater-than-average workload. They are Freda Forster, who made most of the initial contacts with informants, did most of the interviews, and located most of the photographs; Barbara Berry, who expertly transcribed into type almost four hundred pages directly from the tape recordings; and Geoff Lester, who edited and prepared the text for publication.

The majority of the photographs reproduced here have been lent for copying over the last four years and are in the Group's archive. Others have been lent specially for this book. Specific thanks are due to David and Marilyn Bentley, Eric Brassington, Joan Crowder, Betty Dexter, John Francis, Frances and Ernest Hope, Annie Marshall, Bill Slaney, Bessie Thorpe, Gordon Thorpe and Mildred Witham. The photograph of Josiah Greatorex's grocer's shop on Main Street is from the collection of John Wright of Elton, and that of Frank Blackwell's butcher's shop on East Bank is from the collection of Michael Greatorex, who now lives in Tamworth. Thanks are due also to the many others who have loaned photographs which we have not been able to include.

The line drawings are by Joe Kewin, and the cover picture was specially painted by Bill Kirby. Colour prints (42cm by 30cm) and cards based on the painting are available from Winster Post Office.

Finally, we would like to acknowledge the award of a Millennium 'Awards for All' grant, without which it would not have been possible to publish the book in this form. A 'talking-book' version is also available.

Winster Local History Group
Oral History Project

LESLIE BACON. The Bacon family has long connections with Winster. Both Les's father and grandfather lived in the village. Les was born in 1929, attended Winster school and was apprenticed as a wheelwright in Darley Bridge when he was fourteen. He now lives in Hunstone House with his wife, Grace. His brother, Wilf, lives nearby.

HAROLD BARNSLEY was born in Winster in 1919. He lived on the Flat, East Bank, where there were several other Barnsley households - as Harold says, 'No money but plenty of property'. In 1940 he was captured at Dunkirk and spent the next five years as a prisoner of war. After an emotional return to Winster he married Edith Hayes from Matlock, then began working for his father as a builder, and later set up on his own as a painter and decorator. On his retirement he and Edith moved to Matlock.

BERT BOAM was born in Winster (as were his father and grandfather) in 1909 in the Post Office House. He was one of seven children. They were, in order, Winifred, Randolph, Bert, Harold, Hedley, Marjorie and Evelyn. Bert has very clear memories of village life from an early age and has a gift for describing them and for telling stories in an exciting way. At various times he was a gardener at Oddo, a farmhand, a quarryman, a blacksmith, a lorry driver and a lead miner. At Mill Close Mine his skill as a certified 'fireman' meant that he could set and detonate explosives. In 1939 he married Hilda Poundall, from nearby Bonsall, and set up home with her there, eventually buying land and establishing a farm, which is now run by his son, Philip.

HEDLEY BOAM. Numbered fifth of seven children, Hedley was born in 1915 and lived above the Post Office in Main Street. His parents, Ernest and Annie, moved the family to what is now Smithy House, Main Street. Formerly, a second-hand clothes shop, it was run by Annie and Ernest as a fish, chip and wet fish shop, and they also provided a taxi service. Later Hedley added a milk round. In 1950 Hedley married Joan Welch from Darley Dale, and took over the running of the shop until his retirement in 1976. Hedley died in August 1999.

DORIS BRASSINGTON [née Newton], known as 'Dolly' and wife of Ben, was born on West Bank in Winster in 1905. She was married in 1929 from Bank House in Woolley's Yard, her parents being caretakers of the Bank in Main Street. With her husband she moved to Woodland View on the Flat, where their children, Eileen and Eric, were brought up. After Ben's death Dolly moved into the cottage behind Woodland View, now known as Brassington Cottage. In 1982 she moved to Matlock to live with her daughter. She died in January 1999.

ASA COOPER was born at Rockhurst Farm, Aldwark, in 1938. He is the third of sixteen children. In 1965 he met Sylvia Stubbs in a pub in Brassington. They married in April 1967 and moved soon after to their present home at Bank Top, Winster. Starting in a small way and by gradually buying land and rearing cattle, he was able to follow in his family's farming footsteps. Sylvia and Asa have four children – Gill, Asa (known as 'Sam'), Susan and James.

MAVIS CORKER [née Wilson], born 1921, has lived all her life at Carpenter's Cottage, Main Street. Her father, Frederick George Wilson, was the local joiner and undertaker. Mavis married James Watts in 1942, and they had two sons. James died in 1959, and in 1974 she married Thomas Corker. Thomas died in 1979.

EILEEN CROWDER [née Brassington], the eldest child of Ben and Dolly, was born in 1931. In 1961 she married John Crowder, and they now live in Matlock.

BETTY DEXTER [née Greatorex], an only child and now in her 70s, was born at Hillcrest [now Chimney Cottage] on the Flat. Her grandmother sold sweets and vegetables from Hillcrest and kept their two horses in the adjoining front stables. When she was one year old her father died, and the family moved with grandma to the house now named Mia Casa on West Bank, where the business continued and a newsagent's was added. After the death of her first husband, Harry Brandon, Betty met and in 1967 married Ernest Dexter, a lorry driver from Nottingham. On her mother's death she took over the running of the shop until her retirement in 1989.

MARION DRINKALL [née Wild] was born in 1927 at Vernon House, Main Street. In 1951 she married David Drinkall from Eagle Tor, and they had two children. They now live in Matlock.

DOROTHY ('DOT') FEARN [née Walker] was born in 1924. Her father, George, was a pork butcher, who sold from his shop at the bottom of East Bank, now known as Market House. Dot married Richard Fearn in 1946, and for twelve years they were landlord and landlady at the Bowling Green. Their children, Gill and Paul, live in Winster. Dot now lives at Stanfree House, Main Street.

MURIEL GOULD [née Ashcroft] was born in Manchester in 1934. She came to Winster on 1 September 1939 as an evacuee. She lived with Nancy and George Gregory at Pembroke House [now Brae Cottage] on East Bank until she returned home in 1944. In 1955 she married Eric Gould, and they now have three children and four grandchildren. Muriel is still an occasional visitor to Winster Primitive Methodist Chapel.

GLADYS HARDY [née Fern] was born in Bonsall in 1905. She was married to Michael William ('Bill') Hardy in 1928, and they lived in Bonsall for a while, until Bill broke his leg in an accident at Mill Close Mine, after which they moved in with his parents in Woolley's Yard. With Bill off work for nine months and the couple living on £2 a week compensation, they rented Dale View [now Forge Cottage] on East Bank, for 5/6d per week. When Bill died in 1962, Gladys, with her daughter Elveen, moved to Tomkins Cottage, Main Street. In 1982, after a fall, Gladys moved to live with her daughter in Matlock.

STAN HEATHCOTE was born in Bradbourne in 1939. He arrived in Winster, aged fifteen, in the back of the furniture removal van, with his brother, half-brother and aunt. Ashton House, their new home on West Bank, had been a shop, selling sweets and cigarettes. Stan has always been a farm labourer, working mostly for Cartwright's at the Holly Bush, which was once a farm as well as a pub. He was forced into retirement through rheumatism and ill health, and still lives in Ashton House.

VIN HODGKINSON, son of Fred and Tamar, was born in Winster in 1913. He and his father ran a shop in Main Street, which was rebuilt after it burned to the ground in 1933. They sold bicycles, motorbikes, greengrocery and wet fish. They also had a garage, with a petrol pump outside the shop. In the 1930s Fred taught Vin to wire farms and houses and to build and repair radios. Vin later sold televisions. He started a tennis club, a taxi service and a dancing school. In the 1950s he organised dances at the Burton Institute, and helped with the revival of the Winster Morris team. In 1997 Vin was the first person to be interviewed by Winster Local History Group for their Oral History Project. He died later that year.

ERNEST HOPE was born at Hillside View, West Bank, in 1919. His brother, Stan, lived there until recently. The middle child of two brothers and two sisters, Ernest has always lived in Winster. His father, George, a Winster man, married Annie Flint from Bole Hill. Ernest's first job on leaving school at thirteen was making wreaths for a firm in Matlock. Then he went into farming and retired at the age of sixty-three. Snow was on the ground in February 1947 when he married Frances Bateman, whose parents farmed on the Headlands and Islington Lane, Winster. They have a daughter, June.

GRANVILLE JOHNSON, born 1924 in Youlgreave, is the eldest son and third of the five children of Horace, a farmer. In 1937 Horace settled with his family at Stoop Farm [The Old Angel], opposite Winster Market House. Granville helped work the farm, and later the family diversified into fluorspar and barytes. He married Mary Malony, and they had four daughters. Granville worked for some time at Enthoven's lead smelting works.

ANNIE MARSHALL [née Brindley] was born in 1915 in Youlgreave. She met Stanley on 'a monkey run', and they married in 1939. They lived with their in-laws, Frank and Ada Marshall, who lived at Rock View [now Pinfold Cottage] on East Bank, later renting a home of their own at Rockview Cottage, from Josiah Greatorex, the owner of the shop in Main Street. Annie and Stanley had one daughter. Stanley died in 1993, and Annie now lives in Darley Dale.

JOHN MILLWARD, born 1936, lived at Delph Cottage, East Bank, until 1938, when his family moved to Sunnyside on the Main Street. He began his working life as a sawyer for Gregory's wood yard at Darley Dale, but worked mostly as a farm labourer at Birchover. He was a true countryman, and to take a walk with him was a real learning experience. In September 1992 John was interviewed and recorded by Mair Walters as part of a student project on the history of Heathcote House. The recording was kindly made available to the History Group. John died in December 1992.

MILAN PROKOP, was born in Brno, Czechoslovakia, in 1926. He came to Winster, as a refugee in 1948, where he was billeted at Winster Hall, Main Street. He married Brenda Hawksworth in Matlock in 1950. Her father, Theophilus Hawksworth, was a saddler with a shop on Main Street, at the bottom of West Bank [now Holmlea]. They had a daughter, Diana, who now lives in America. In 1957 Milan and Brenda emigrated to Canada, but Brenda couldn't settle, so they returned in 1962 to live at Hill Cottage, West Bank, where Milan still lives. Brenda died in 1993.

BILL SLANEY lives at Denver House, Main Street. He was born in Youlgreave in 1913. His parents died when he was in his teens, and he moved to Winster in 1939. He married Annie Stone, a well known pianist and the daughter of the landlord and landlady of the Crown. Bill and Annie's first home was Greenlees Cottage, next to the Post Office.

AMY SLATER was born in 1930 in Youlgreave. After living on a remote farm on Gratton Moor she was almost eight when the family moved to Stoop Farm, Main Street, Winster. She was the fourth of five children. Her father, Horace Johnson, was a representative on the Parish and Rural District Councils and served as a local preacher. Amy worked hard on the farm, even at times shovelling fluorspar and barytes. She met her future husband, Dennis, from Whiteholmes Farm, when as a young man he was employed by her father. Their son, Gordon, lives with his family on East Bank. Today Amy and her family are inspirational in the running of the Wesleyan Reform Chapel.

MARJORIE STOKER was born in Cuba in 1908. She came to England with her mother when she was about four years old, following the death of her father. She is the widow of Arthur 'Desmond' Stoker, who first came to Winster in 1934 to take over from James Fletcher as village doctor. They married in 1936. In 1939 Desmond joined the armed services, and when he returned they built up a flourishing practice, the surgery beginning in the house. They had twins, Andrew and Simon. Marjorie lives in Winster on West Bank.

PHYLLIS TAYLOR [née Marshall] was born in 1917 at E. A. Marshall & Sons, a printing, photography and stationery business opposite the Market House, Winster. Her grandfather, Albert Marshall, died in 1918, and when her father, also Albert Marshall, returned from the Great War, he took over the family business. Many old photographs and postcards of Winster are the work of these two. Phyllis left school at fifteen to help her grandmother run the shop. She met George Taylor, from Bonsall, and they married and rented Jasmine Cottage, in Pump Lane. It was after Molly, their first daughter, was born, that they moved to Liskeard, Cornwall, where Phyllis still lives.

HAROLD THOMAS was born in 1907. His grandfather, Stephen Thomas, came from Cornwall in 1878 to set up the 'Jumbo' pump at Mill Close Mine. Most of Stephen's children, including Paul, Harold's father, also worked in the mine. Annie Thomas, Harold's cousin, was author of the poem 'The Brave Winster Boys', about the men from the village who served in the Great War. Harold now lives in Allestree, Derby, with his wife Kath.

BESSIE THORPE [née Boden] was born in 1914. Her father, Walter, established the family bakery in 1913 at the top of Pump Lane [The Old Bakehouse]. He later became treasurer of the Parish Council. When she was only thirteen Bessie's mother died suddenly, and Bessie had to take over the running of the bakery with her father. She played an active part in village affairs and she succeeded Miss Buxton in organising the running of the Wesleyan Reform Chapel, East Bank. She married Clifford in 1951 and moved to Matlock, where they raised their son, Michael. Bessie died in December 1997.

MARGARET TOMLINSON was born in 1922 and came to Winster from Sheffield at the time of her marriage to her first husband, Eric Roper, in 1942. During the First World War Eric's father had started farming at the top of Winster Bank and was gradually able to build up the farm by buying more land. Margaret and Eric had four children - Jane, Andrew ('Jim'), William and Ian. Jim now runs the farm and is King of Winster Morris. Margaret lives in Winster with her second husband, Charlie.

LOUIS [Alojz] VINCENT was born in 1930 in Lipovljani, Yugoslavia [Croatia]. He arrived in Winster in 1948 as a displaced person, and was housed, with about forty others, in Winster Hall. They were employed at Friden Brickworks until 1951, after which they were free to seek other employment. Louis met Eunice Stone at a dance in the Burton Institute and they married in 1949. They bought their present house on East Bank for £75, having to borrow £25 from Eunice's brother for the deposit. They have four children.

JACK WALKER was born in 1926 and lived in Manchester. On leaving the army he came to Winster in 1956 and married Bessie Greatorex. Jack is an ardent supporter of Manchester United and is a regular at the Miners' Standard.

ANNE WALTERS was born in 1940 in Rose Cottage (now Carpenter's Cottage) on the Flat, East Bank, Winster. Her father was Bill Barnsley and her mother was Bertha, who for many years played the organ in the Primitive Methodist Chapel just behind their house. Over the years Anne has been involved in many aspects of village life, but most people know her as the person who worked in Mosley's (later Yates') village stores for 40 years, until she and her husband, Roy, moved to a bungalow three miles away in Darley Dale in 1997.

ROY WALTERS was born in 1935 in nearby Birchover. He was demobbed in 1956 and moved to Winster when he married Anne in 1961. At first they lived in Buxton Cottage on West Bank, then in the cottage adjoining Anne's mother, Bertha, on the Flat. They occupied the whole house when Bertha died. For many years Roy worked at Shand's, an engineering company in Darley Dale. He and Anne have two children. They are still members of Winster Primitive Methodist Church.

TOM WIGLEY was born in 1915 in Hognaston, and arrived in Winster aged twelve, first to live at Stoop Farm [The Old Angel] on Main Street. In about 1932 his family moved to Painter's Way Farm. He married Eva Webster, from Elton, and they had two sons. Tom died in 1999.

MILDRED WITHAM was born in 1920 at Croft End, East Bank. She is the eldest and only girl of the three children of Dorothy and William Witham. The family moved to Westhills Farm when Mildred was three or four years old, and they stayed there until she was twelve, when they made their home at 5 Woolley's Yard [now Musk Cottage]. Mildred still lives there. At one time she was the Treasurer of the British Legion, and today she is involved in all kinds of charity work, particularly for the Burton Institute and St John's Church.

DEREK (born 1933) and PAULINE WOOD (born 1939) sold their home and business at Elton in 1972 and bought Winster Hall for £9,750, as extended family accommodation. The Hall became a pub after 1984 when Pauline was granted a licence to sell alcohol. Six years later they sold it as a going concern to Mr Warboys. Mr Burrows was the owner when the pub closed. Many people have happy memories of Winster Hall as a 'village' pub and a centre of social life. Pauline and Derek now live in Elton.

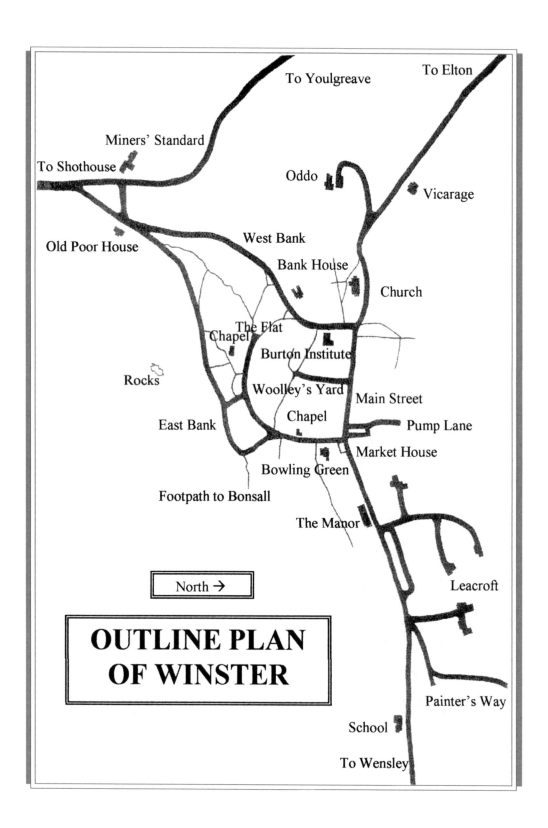

To Youlgreave

To Elton

Miners' Standard

To Shothouse

Oddo

Vicarage

Old Poor House

West Bank

Bank House

Church

The Flat

Chapel

Burton Institute

Rocks

Woolley's Yard

Main Street

Chapel

East Bank

Pump Lane

Market House

Bowling Green

Footpath to Bonsall

The Manor

North →

Leacroft

OUTLINE PLAN
OF WINSTER

Painter's Way

School

To Wensley

The entries are arranged in the form of a tour round the village, starting at the end of Main Street nearest Wensley. Go along the left side of Main Street, up and down West Bank, back along the other side of Main Street (taking in Pump Lane), up East Bank (branching right at the fork on to the Flat), and back via the other branch of East Bank. The memories cover a wide span of years, during which shops closed or changed hands. First, though, two general descriptions of Winster's thriving commercial past...

Main Street, outside the shop of Josiah Greatorex, Grocer, c. 1907.

When blacksmiths made their own nails.

When my mother was a child there was everything in the village. There was the blacksmith's, and the blacksmith made his own nails and everything. There were two saddlers. If you come down West Bank, there's Mrs Adams at the corner. She had sweets - this is while I've been a child. You come down to where Roland Corfield lives, and that was the Co-op. Opposite there, where Stan Heathcote lives, that was a shop, and when my mother was young they baked bread every day there. You come down to the corner and there was the butcher's, but before it was the butcher's it used to be a draper's shop. I can remember my mother buying my clothes from there. Opposite was a saddler's and shoe shop. He didn't make the shoes, he sold shoes. He made saddles, horse collars, and repaired them and all that. Then there was another butcher's, and you got down to where Brian Long lives, and that was Hodgkinson's when I was a child. She had a sweet shop and she sold bread and cakes at the far end, and, joined to it, was the bigger shop with cycles. Then they got into selling radios, and when televisions came Vinny Hodgkinson sold them, too. And they had two petrol pumps outside, two petrol pumps on the footpath. Then you went where Macdonald's garage is now, where Mrs Ball lives now. Tom Edward Gregory lived there, and he run the garage at the back there. He had a petrol pump at the bottom of the yard on the street. Where Pam Lamb lives, that was another saddler's, that was John Rowland's. I can see John Rowland now! He used to come out and sit on the windowsill, and we used to go and talk to him when we were children. He always told us funny tales. There was Boden's bakehouse in Pump Lane, and Robert Thorpe's shop where Glyn Yates is. Then there'd be the Angel. Market Cottage, Printer Marshall lived there. He had a printer's shop. Then, next door to his printer's shop, Mavis Corker's was the joiner and undertaker's, and that was Fred Wilson. Next to the joiner's shop was a sweet shop that Mrs Wilson ran. We used to call there on our way to school for aniseed balls and all sorts of stuff. Of course, there was Gilding's shop. When my mother's uncle lived where Skinner now lives, he had a tailor's shop. He was a tailor. He used to make the riding habits for people at Oddo and all round, the farmers. [Mildred Witham]

Winster's many shops.

Starting at West Bank, Betty Brandon's was a sweet shop, and she sold papers. 'Richfield' was the Co-op. Then on Main Street, where Sandra's Hairdressing shop is, there was a shoe shop called Hawksworth's Saddlery, which afterwards became Roland Marshall's wallpaper shop. Opposite that, on the corner, was George Will Stone. That was a butcher's shop for a long time. He did his own slaughtering somewhere. Another butcher's, Blackwell's, was a few doors on, and then where the Grays live was the chip shop. Where Longs live is where Vinny Hodgkinson had his shop. He sold radios, TVs, bicycles at one side, and sweets, confectionery, bread at the other side. Then you have the Bank House. That was the Royal Bank of Scotland, but before that it was Williams Deacons and William's and Glyn's. You have the Post Office after the Bank. On the opposite side, 'Beech View' was Mrs Denham's haberdashery - cottons, embroidery silks, like a draper's. 'Moot House', where the bus stop is, Stan Boam had a butcher's shop there. After Stan Boam gave up, Fletcher from Matlock butchered there. Where Gillian Fearn's house is now, that used to be a butcher's shop owned by George Walker. Where Tomlinsons live, that was the bakery. Then there was Harold Mosley's, where I worked. It used to be Thorpe's before that, and now Glyn has it. Where Laurie Warren lives used to be Evelyn Webster's little shop. She sold everything - silks, pots, dishes, books, boots, shoes, clothes, everything, and the dairy at the side. Where Mavis Corker lives there used to be a little sweet shop. Then Gilding's, which was hardware, ironmongers, paraffin, fireworks, everything. I got a lot of my wedding presents there. We were married in 1961, and people said, 'Pop down to Mrs Gilding and her sister Dorothy and pick whatever you want.' Mr Gilding used to go round with a van selling things. Going up East Bank there was Mrs Hodgkinson, who sold fancy goods, small amounts of groceries, paraffin, buttons, elastic, cottons, potatoes, carrots and sweets. Salt of the earth she was. Just nip down to the bottom and you could get it, quick. Where Peter Bateman lives Toby Thorpe always used to charge batteries on that Bank, at Ephraim House. And Mrs Scriven used to sell crisps, biscuits and sweets from the house, like a little shop. [Anne Walters]

Main Street from the East

Ivy Cottage. Dentist.

Dentist came to Winster once a week on a Thursday afternoon – Mr Blythe. He had a room in next house past the Manor [Ivy Cottage], and there were a board outside with his name on. I remember my mother having her teeth out there. [Ernest Hope]

The Manor. Private Hotel.

At one time Harry Fengel owned the Manor, which was called 'The Rendezvous.' The villagers called it 'The Den' [of Iniquity]. It was a private hotel, used mainly by Sheffield businessmen, who brought their wives (or someone else's). Village people didn't use the place. In those days gambling was illegal, but they used to play cards there. My dad used to take meat on a Saturday, and sometimes he would stop and join in. My mother used to play hell! The police raided it once. People ran in all different directions. My mum said to dad, 'George, it's a good job you've got your slops [apron] on!' He was able to say he was delivering the meat. There were tennis courts there, too, and they charged 2d an hour to play. My teacher at Winster, Frances Williams, used to pay for the court, and I played there with her. [Dot Fearn]

> Winster Wisdom: 'Big bills you canna pay,
> little bills you dunna bother with.'

Newholme. Milk.

John Isaac Greatorex lived there. He kept a few cows down Leacroft and sold milk round the village. He used to hook the churn on a dandy – that was a round steel contraption with two wheels with rubber tyres. That's how he used to do it. [Bert Boam]

Market House. Pot sales.

I don't remember ever hearing the Curfew Bell in Winster. Only bell as I know was when they used to bring brown potware to Market House on a Saturday night, because people used to make their own bread in them days, and they used to have what they called 'pancheons'. It were a big brown thing, like, and there were such a lot of brownware, stewpots, and everything. It were all brown then. They used to come with a covered wagon. They used to bring this brownware and then set it out, and then they used to ring bell for people to go down on a Saturday night. They used to sell it like auction. [Bert Boam]

Moot House. Butcher.

That's where Butcher Boam had his meat shop. Butcher Boam didn't sell any pork at all, only beef, but Dorothy Walker's dad he only had pork. Blackwell, he sold pork and beef. So there were three butchers in Winster when I were a lad. [Bert Boam]

The Old Brewhouse. Village Stores.

First it belonged to 'Siah Greatorex, then Jess Burton started working for him, and then eventually Mr Greatorex retired and Burton took over, so that's how it got to Burton's shop, through him starting working there. So he took it over finally. Jess Burton his name was. [Bert Boam]

Denver House. Butcher.

Where I'm living now, it used to be a pork butcher's shop. Up in the attic you've got all the hooks in the beams where they used to hang all the bacon, hams and what have you. If you look over the top of the front window you can see where there's been the board with the shop name, little wooden plugs where they plugged it in to the wall. When George Will Stone lived across at the Crown he said he used to hear a little engine going in this building here, and it was the owner of the butcher's shop making his sausage meat. It was a little engine - pump, pump, pump - you could hear it going. [Bill Slaney]

Back of Denver House. Cobbler.

Old Mr Denham was up the Crown Yard. If you notice, where Bill Slaney lives there's some little sheds, and he used to do his cobbling in there. That was Mr Denham. [Dot Fearn]

Post Office. Post Office and Chemist.

The Post Office was owned by Ernest Heathcote. You always had to raise your hat to him in those days. He let us rent the Post Office for accommodation, because he lived at Mooresfold. But all the business of the Post Office was run by Ernest Heathcote. When I were a boy there wasn't a telephone in none of the villages round about, only Winster - that was the only place that had got a telephone. The message used to come to Winster, and they used to write it out on a sheet of paper and call it a telegram. We lived in the Post Office House, so different ones in the family - it all depended who was available - used to have to take a telegram as far as Pikehall, and sometimes at seven o'clock at night, and walk it to Pikehall, and sometimes go to Gratton, and take all the telegrams round the villages - Birchover, Elton and Wensley. You had to walk with all those, and in winter time. [Bert Boam]

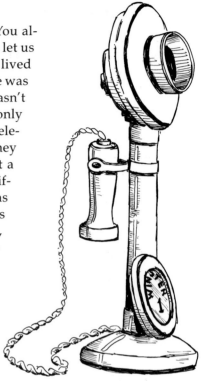

'the only place that had got a telephone'

Post Office. Post Office and Chemist.

Ernest Heathcote kept the Post Office and he was a chemist. He just failed to be a doctor, so he was a chemist . When I was a child you could get all sorts from Heathcote there at the Post Office, all kinds of medicines. He used to make his own remedies up. He kept all kinds of things like that. I can remember having toothache and my mother saying, 'Go down to the Post Office and get some tincture of myrrh and put that on it.' And it used to numb it. [Mildred Witham]

Post Office. Post Office and Chemist.

I remember the Post Office when I was a little girl. I used to go and do errands for the two Miss Browns, and on Saturday morning I would either clean the silver or top-and-tail the gooseberries. Then I used to go each night from school to see if there were any errands or any telegrams. I used to get a shilling a week for doing that. As you walked in, the Post Office side was to the left and to the right was the drapery side. In front, as you walked in, was a chemistry counter with all the aspirins and things like that on. Miss Brown - Lily this was - she used to sit on a chair, and when there was no-one in the shop she would put her leg on the counter. They had their specific jobs. One was the postmistress and the other used to do the housekeeping. Joan Wild, in very first memories, answered the phone. She eventually became a switchboard operator elsewhere. [Marion Drinkall]

The Old Bank House. Bank.

Newtons used to live there, and the bank used to open about once a week. The bank were part of the house. It was the front part of the house, and Newtons used to come out into Woolley's Yard, and they had to go up Woolley's Yard to get into theirs, because the bank was separate. Now it's joined into one. You can go in off the street where the railings are and you can come out at Woolley's Yard, because it's all one now. But Newtons lived there then. [Bert Boam]

Tor House. Bicycles, electrical goods, etc.

The business was in the Main Street. At first my father was manufacturing his own bicycles and selling them. He used to have all us kids cleaning the frames, making them shine like silver. Then he used to enamel them - dip them in an enamel trough, hang them up and let them drain, and then they used to put them into this big gas stove about eight feet or ten feet square. They used to be stove enamelled, and they used to have to be dipped again and go through it again. Then he used to line the tubes with a line, and he used to put his transfer on the front. He used to make his own bicycles. Then these 'ere big firms come on, like Raleigh - well, Hercules more than anything. They were selling them at about £5 19s 6d. Well, he couldn't make 'em for that price, you see, so he packed up and bought them from wholesalers. Everybody in Winster, presumably, rode bikes to work. There were hundreds of bikes in Winster, must have been. We used to have greengrocery and wet fish and sold bicycles and motorbikes. Then my father used to have a bit of a garage where he used to repair Ford cars and motorbikes and that. I was decarbonising motorbikes at nine years old. We got burnt out in 1933, burnt down. All the lot went up. After we were burnt out we went and lived down with my Uncle Jack Rouse at Ivy Cottage across here, on the main road, where the builder lives now. He's a builder, isn't he? We were there twelve months, until the house was done. It was rebuilt. The fire was on the 20th December. It was £400 under-insured, because my father hadn't had time to insure his Christmas stuff. A lot of people lost some Christmas presents then, you know! It took the fire engine between an hour and two hours to come. It were burnt out, practically, by the time they got here. All they could do was save next door's property. They were lucky they could put it out. We had one petrol pump there and one oil cabinet. All they could do was spray it with water to stop it catching fire. [Vin Hodgkinson]

Farriers. Butcher.

I think once it had something to do with Arthur Heathcote with his glass. It was like a store place for quite a long while, and as time went on Frank Blackwell, that kept the Bowling Green, he turned it into a butcher's shop, and he used to sell his meat from there as time went by. [Bert Boam]

Smithy House. Fish and Chips.

Ernest Heathcote were a very careful sort of man, and he'd got all this money. You know that I was bred and born at the Post Office House, but we didn't keep the Post Office. Now, Ernest Heathcote kept the Post Office. So my mother was going to have this chip shop up the Main Street in the place that had been Gregory's second-hand clothes shop before - that's why the big window was in – and they do say that once upon a time it used to be a smithy - this is how things have been all altered. Well, my mother bought it off Ernest Heathcote, and he lent her the money without any interest, to help her, because we'd come out of the Post Office House. I couldn't say for sure how much, but it wouldn't be ever so much, perhaps £150 or £200. Might not be as much as that, I don't know for sure, but they wouldn't be ever so dear then. So that's how my mother and dad got that chip shop. Then dad, he was working at the quarry, and mum always wanted him to have a business and pack the quarrying up, and she persuaded him to buy a little pony and trap and go out with wet fish. He used to go to Elton, Youlgreave and different places with wet fish. He used to go to Darley Station every morning and meet the 7.45 milk train, because all the farmers then, same as Winster, these bigger farmers, used to have to take their milk to Darley Station and catch train and send it all off in churns. Dad used to meet the 7.45 train, and sometimes we had fish from Grimsby and sometimes we had it from Fleetwood, because they quoted you different prices in those days. If it was cheaper at Fleetwood we'd have it from there. Dad always met that train at Darley Dale, and it used to come in great big wooden boxes, and there used to be a layer of fish and a layer of ice, and none of it was frozen. Today it's frozen out at sea, so you don't get it fresh like we got it. And it was beautiful! I always say that with it being frozen there's so much of the taste goes out of it. [Bert Boam]

Smithy House. Fish and Chips.

Hedley Boam 'ad fish an chip shop. We use go in theer on a Sat'day night - fish, chips, eggs an bread an butter an coffee. An y'd be in theer 'til one o'clock in a mornin'. Ah use bring 'im potatoes, ah did. Mosleys, up theer up Pikehall, we use go fer um. We use say, 'Way gooin fer a load a 'tatoes tonight. Are yer fit?' [Stan Heathcote]

The Old Butcher's. Draper and Butcher.

There were a draper's shop, Sam Hodgkinson, right on the corner, but if you wanted a suit you had to go to Matlock for made to measure. But old draper's shop, it was a big window. These clothes used to be hung up in window and they seemed to be there for years. I dunna think he had a lot o' trade. Then he left, and it would be George Will Stone, he had a butcher's shop there. [Tom Wigley]

Winster Wisdom: 'Eaten bread is soon forgotten.'

West Bank

Ashton House. Bread and Ice Cream.

Where Stanley Heathcote lives, that was a shop, a lovely shop. They used to bake their own bread, make their own ice cream, and they sold sweets and groceries. A Mrs Lomas it was. I think she had a niece, a Miss Durden, and this Miss Durden had a son. His name was Billy, and I remember going as a child and they were making this ice cream. [Betty Dexter]

Richfield. Co-op.

Hedley Bacon was the manager, as I recall. You remember the 'divi' days? [Marion Drinkall]

West Bank House. Smithy.

Where your garage is [West Bank House], Mr Vincent used to be there. He had that as a smithy. This was when I was a little girl. And sometimes the horses would be queuing down West Bank waiting to be shod. [Betty Dexter]

Heaton House. Blacksmith and Wheelwright.

That was the blacksmith's, just down below Dexter's. In that jitty there, that's where you used to go. He was a wheelwright – Jess Wild - and that's where he had his shop. [Bert Boam]

Mia Casa. Sweets and Newspapers.

First of all it was Betty Greatorex's grandma, Mrs Adams. Then Betty took over the shop, and it was known as Betty Brandon's. And then later it was known as Dexter's. She used to have newspapers, sweets, crisps, biscuits and all things like that. [Anne Walters]

Shed opposite Wayside. Fish and Chips.

My mother bought that house where the chip shop was in Winster Street [Smithy House]. But before my mum had that, we had that little place like a shed on Chip Shop Hill. That's where we began. We started doing fish and chips in Winster in that little place. There was only one copper, and you had to get your heat with the coal. There wasn't any gas. We had a storm lantern hung up for a light. We did chips as well as fish. There was, like, proper little chip bags, like a boat thing, and they used to be piled up for one pennyworth of chips. Fish was seven for a shilling or 2d each. People used to be queuing for a long way, because it was so small we couldn't do the fish very quickly. [Bert Boam]

Main Street going East, including Pump Lane [now Woodhouse Lane]

Holmlea. Saddler.

The old craftsmen have died off and gone. Same as where my sister lived [Beech View], there was John Rowland, the saddler there. He could make saddles, lay silver in them, same as Theophilus and his shop up here [Holmlea]. He made shoes for you. He specialised in shoes and saddleware, crops and whips, and anything like that. They all died out, you see, and now it's mainly holiday cottages. [John Millward]

Holmlea. Saddler.

That were Theophilus Hawksworth, and he were saddler, and he used to make horses' collars. That was his living. He used to get this straw and just mull it round, and get the leather and put round and stitch it. It was all hand-stitched - he hadn't got a machine. He even used to make footballs, even for same as Matlock Town. They were all leather footballs. There weren't any of these plastic footballs in them days. He used to cut the leather in sections and then hand-stitch it all together. He used to make footballs galore like that. When it was a wet day and you had one of them, oh, it was just like kicking a piece of lead! Today they can keep heading these balls from one to another, but you couldn't in them days, not when it was wet. He used to make anything for horses, and he used to get ever such big sheets

'on a wet day it was like kicking a piece of lead'

of leather come to his place, and cut them out. He made reins for horses and all things in leather. [Bert Boam]

The Courtyard. Paint etc.

Old Arthur Heathcote had a general store there. He used to mix his own paint and all that. Roland Marshall took it over when he died. Arthur sold treacle, putty, glass, wallpaper, tackle, nails, wire, and all sorts of things he sold in there. Had a right good little business. And at one time there was these two hooks in Mrs Gregory's house down the yard where he hung a banner advertising his things, and it's still there what he hung his things on. And it advertised what he was selling. We used to go for treacle. It were 6d for 2lb. We always put 6d in bottom of jar, and he always filled jar up. And he'd say, 'Where's your 6d?' 'It's int' bottom of jar. You'll have to eat treacle for it.' [John Millward]

The Courtyard. Paint etc.

Arthur Heathcote used to sell putty and treacle and soap. You could buy your bars of soap, big bars, and big bars of salt, and everything of that description. As you come down this jitty there, that's where he had his shop, and you used to go for your treacle. He'd cut your glass or anything of that sort. Them were buildings belonging to him. The one they call The Cottage were a shop of his, and then it got turned into a house somehow, and Marshalls lived at it, Ewart Marshall. [Bert Boam]

Old Hall Cottage. Cycle shop.

Tom Edward Gregory had it, and he had a cycle shop. He had petrol pump on the footpath. And they used to sell bicycles and repair them and let them out. They used to let their bicycles out for people to learn on in them days. So he was the bicycle man. [Bert Boam]

Beech View. Saddler.

Where my brother lived, the next one were John Rowland's boot and shoe shop. Yes, and there's still the big window there, I think, isn't there? He had a lovely boot and shoe shop, he did, there, and they were, like, a better class. He used to sell heavy shoes, and in them days there used to be such a lot of nails in, like studs for heavy work. He used to sell all sorts of things like that, John Rowland. A high class boot shop. [Bert Boam]

Glendare. Fish and Chips.

My Granny Holmes was the first person ever to have a chip shop in Winster. Door opened off Main Street, off causeway, and you went up this passage, about a yard wide, and turned left into the back yard. When you landed in the back yard there was a building whitewashed. She had an ordinary copper, the sort what you wash clothes in, and that's how she did her fish and chips. [Bert Boam]

Gable House. Milk.

The Dales were the main suppliers of milk. They delivered from their shop, almost opposite Greatorex's, as it was in those days. It's now Burton's Stores [now The Old Brewhouse], opposite the Hall. Matthew Dale used to bring the milk down in the early days, and then later Ted used to help, on a yoke from the Horsecrofts - bring it down with buckets. And then there used to be the massive filters which it went through and sterilised the buckets - all the ladles, half-pint, pints. There were the milk cans, which were scrupulously clean and all sterilised. Kathleen and I used to take it round at night, round the villagers. We used to knock at the door and people would empty it into their milk jugs. Then you'd take it back and go and get some more. It was always very fresh milk - not pasteurised or anything like that, just fresh milk. [Marion Drinkall]

GB Stores. General Shop.

Thorpes used to keep that shop in my day. It was a general shop, groceries, and they always had someone - Dan Ingham - he worked for Thorpes many, many years, he did, because most of these village shops used to have someone helping them in the shop. [Bert Boam]

Pump Lane. The Old Bakehouse. Baker.

Down Pump Lane was the Bakery. They used to call him Baker Boden. You'd go and get a bag of buns from Baker Boden's. I think they were ha'penny or penny buns. They used to take papers for us up on to the farms, same as the weekly papers, Derbyshire Times and all that. Mum used to pack them up, roll them up and put names on, and Harry Boden, his son, used to take them up on to the farms, because they couldn't get down regular. [Betty Dexter]

Pump Lane. The Old Bakehouse. Baker.

Just below the bakehouse there was a stable, and they kept their horse there, because they used to take the bread to Elton, Wensley and Darley Dale. They had to use the horse every day. And they'd be working - same as Saturday - sometimes until nine o'clock at night, happen, at Darley Bridge with horse and trap in them days. They used to be marvellous at Christmas time. You couldn't believe it! Us lads, you couldn't afford anything, but when you went there, and it come Christmas time, and they'd got all the Christmas cakes in the window, it were lovely! It were all decorated up everywhere, the window, and people used to go on purpose, two or three days before Christmas, to have a look how nice the shops were decorated up in them days. [Bert Boam]

Pump Lane.
Workshop at back of GB Stores. Fish and Chips.

There was another chip shop down Pump Lane, downside of Yates' shop. It were an old cowshed before it were a chip shop, 'cause there used to be a little farm down there. Oh yes, a cowshed there. When you look around there's been a cowshed and a pigsty and all sorts of farm buildings, all where you wouldn't think they'd be. They've all done a little bit with a cow or two, yer know, time back, years back. They've all done a little bit of mining and a little bit of farming. I've heard old uns say they used to do about six hours – a six-hour shift down underground – and then back home o'er top, you know. [Tom Wigley]

The Old Angel. Ice cream.

The Wayne family lived where the Bradburys live now, at the Angel. They were farmers, and Mrs Wayne used to make ice-cream. It was lovely. You used to get a great big one for a penny, and if you took a basin you got more. [Dot Fearn]

Market Cottage. Printer.

Then there were a printer's shop - Marshall's the printer - and he had his printing shop there, and then his house a bit farther joined on to it. The shop was right against The Angel, and they used to sell stationery, ribbons, and all sorts of things then. The wife run that sort of shop, and mister run the printing thing, Marshall's Printers. They use to print magazines and everything like that. Then later on it was Webster's, and they sold all sorts of bits and bobs, such as bobbins of cotton, pencils, envelopes and birthday cards. [Bert Boam]

Market Cottage. Printer.

The family printing business was passed on to my father from his father, who sadly died when my father was in the Great War, 1914. He was presumed missing, presumed killed. Actually he was wounded through his cheeks that shattered all his teeth, and then there was the German surgeon who, he said, was very, very good to him. And he came back again. I was only about a year old. My father took over the business and he was a printer and a photographer. We used to sell toys, all stationery and equipment, Christmas cards, birthday cards, pens, lots of toys, whips and tops, marbles, and meccano. We used to go to Manchester to John Lewis' to get our stock, and a traveller used to come from Derby. The printing business used to do business all over Derbyshire, miles around, everything. [Phyllis Taylor]

Carpenter's Cottage. Sweets and Undertaker.

That was Wilson's shop. Mavis [now Corker], she was born there, and they had this sweet shop. They had marvellous sweets in them days - all these here fancy

'sweet shop and undertaker'

things as you never see today, like aniseed balls. I think you got about perhaps twenty for a ha'penny, and they were all things like that. They did so well because all schoolchildren used to have to go past the house, and they used to get all these here fresh things come in - these great big humbugs and all sorts of things like that. And they were ever so cheap - ha'penny and that - because they were for the schoolchildren - that were reason why. Joining on to it were Mr Freddy Wilson's joiner's shop. That was on the edge of it. It joined on to the toffee shop, really. Mavis Corker's family name was Wilson. Mr Wilson was the joiner, and he made coffins an' all. [Bert Boam]

Carpenter's Cottage. Sweets and Undertaker.

Mr Wilson was the undertaker. They had a little shop, just opposite Frank Sumner's, where Mavis Corker lives. Her mum had this sweet shop and Mr Wilson had joiner's shop next to the sweets, where he made the coffins. [Dot Fearn]

Carpenter's Cottage. Sweets and Undertaker.

There was the sweet shop of Mrs Wilson's next door to Vernon House. It was really two shops, a sweet shop one side and the undertaker's and joinery on the other side. I always find that very peculiar - sweets on one side for the children and a burial parlour for the elderly on the way out. I can remember seeing a baby in its coffin. [Marion Drinkall]

The Old Forge. Tinsmith.

There was also an ironmongers. It were a handy place to go to. It didn't matter what you wanted, you could get it. That went in name o' John Gilding. A very good place, that were. Anything you wanted, and if they 'adna gorrit, they'd gerrit tomorrow. [Tom Wigley]

The Old Forge. Tinsmith.

Gildings had a shop there and they used to sell all sorts, pots, pans, gas mantles, and everything of that sort. At the back of Gilding's he had a workshop. He used to make buckets and even kettles, he did, himself. He were a proper tinsmith, and he used to have great sheets, monstrous sheets, of tin come, like that, and he could make anything - buckets and anything out of tin. He was a proper tinsmith. As time went on they set up a Ford and went to Elton and round these farms with paraffin and everything of that description. [Bert Boam]

The Old Forge. Tinsmith.

John Gilding sold nails, chisels, screwdrivers, hammers, bolts, anything you wanted. Wire netting, barbed wire, chamber pots, cartridges, guns - he was a gunsmith as well. He was a right good un, and he's int' churchyard now. He'd put your guttering up [at Heathcote House]. He'd do your roof up himself. He'd do all the work himself. He was an odd job man, like, gardening, anything. He put paths round the garden, you know, those concrete paths round the garden -

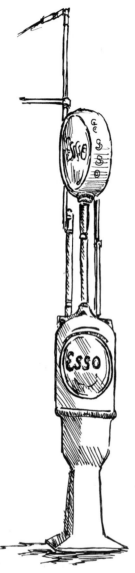

that would be int' early 40s - and he buttressed that wall. I remember him doing it, put buttresses up. [John Millward]

The Old Forge. Tinsmith.

Gildings had the shop, the ironmongers. We used to play in their backyard, where they had a sandpit. With Nancy's father doing all kinds of plumbing work and things like that, they used to have all sand at the top, and Nancy and I used to have our buckets and spades and really enjoy it. I remember that you went in at the door and turned immediately right into the shop. There was the counter there. The living room was at the back. It was absolutely beautiful - pots, pans, all kinds of things, really. I can just remember pots and pans and cleaning things, dolly pegs, dolly tubs, and all the things that were used during that time. They used to go out twice a week and load the lorry up with all the things on. During the week it had to be all done each time and taken away, because the lorry was used for the other work that John Gilding did. There's like a barn or a house in the garden at the back. I believe he used that as his workshop. [Marion Drinkall]

Leacroft Garage. Petrol.

This was bought by Harry Fengel, who also owned the Manor. Tommy Todd (Toddy) used to serve petrol there, and he lived for a time in the flat above. So there were three places you could buy petrol in Winster – Hodgkinson's, Putty Gregory's and Fengel's. [Dot Fearn]

East Bank

Market House. Butcher.

'there were three places you could buy petrol'

Gill's kitchen [Market House] was the butcher's shop. I only said to Gill the other day, at Christmas it was, when she was peeling potatoes, 'Where you're standing, when we lived here, there'd be about 10 pigs' heads hanging up with oranges in.' There used to be a Miss Walker (no relation), who lived opposite the Burton Institute, and it used to upset her to see these pigs' heads with oranges in. She used to call my dad a very cruel man. My dad used to rear the pigs where the ladies toilets are. We had a little bit of ground up there with pigsties. He used to rear them and kill them and do all the making up, and my mum did too. In the back kitchen there was a sausage machine, another mixing machine and a big copper. They used to boil the brawn and make all sorts. They used to boil all the pigs' feet and heads and pull all the pork off, away from the skin and gristle, and put it in big pots, and my mum used to put a plate on top with a weight and let it set. When my dad used to kill the pigs he used a humane killer. He'd shoot the pig and then cut the throat, and he'd have me holding a bucket with a big spoon, stirring all the time so that it wouldn't congeal, so as he could make his black puddings. He had the shop, also a horse and cart, and he used to cart it round Elton and Birchover. Sometimes I went with him on his rounds. This particular day he'd taken his meat to this farm and left me sat in the cart. All at once this man set off blowing his trumpet, and the horse didn't like it, so it took off with me right up Birchover and up to Stanton. Then there was Mr Marsden, the road man. He grabbed the horse's reins, jumped in the cart and drove me back down to Eagle Tor. So my dad wasn't very pleased with this man on the trumpet. He gave him tuppence to let him deliver his meat and not strike up with the cornet, and that was the end of that. He didn't like music at all, the horse. He didn't like mouth organs - they used to upset him - and he didn't like donkeys! [Dot Fearn]

East Hill. Butcher.

This is where Blackwells first had their butcher's shop. Then they moved down near Main Street, opposite the Market House, underneath that archway. Then they moved on to Main Street, where Heathcote had a paint shop once upon a

Frank Blackwell's Butcher's Shop, East Bank.

time [Farriers]. Then Blackwell got hold of it and made it into a butcher's shop. Then for a while he kept the Bowling Green as well as run the shop. [Bert Boam]

Outbuilding next to Edge Cottage. Cobbler.

Then there was Mr Kemp, who lived up East Bank, in Edge Cottage, where the Burton girls were born. He was quite a high-class cobbler. He was very good. He used to tickle me. I used to go and watch him. I was fascinated. He'd get these tacks and throw a handful into his mouth, so that he wouldn't have to keep picking them up out of the tin. He'd just pick one out of his mouth and banged it into the shoe. [Dot Fearn]

Kingsfield Cottage. General Shop.

Miss Winfield had a lovely little shop. She used to sell all sorts there – sweets, ribbons. And at Christmas time she used to really decorate it up - such as sugar pigs, sweet watches, and chocolate Santa Clauses. [Bert Boam]

Hunstone House. General Shop.

And then Hunstone House - that was Mrs Joseph Newton. No relation to us [i.e. Dolly Brassington, née Newton] at all. The little shop at the corner, that was. If you didn't want to go down in the village shopping, she sold all sorts of things - groceries, haberdashery, towels, cotton, wool, everything. [Dolly Brassington]

No 1 the Flat. Sweets.

It were just a little room belonging to the house. Mrs Allen sold all sorts of sweets there, fancy things, like sherbet – two or three different colours – and a piece of liquorice so you could suck it. [Bert Boam]

Bank Cottage. Greengrocer.

And then just on the road from there was Mr Rains, and he had a little greengrocer's shop there, on the Flat. But mostly he took it round the villages with a pony and a little flat cart. And he was known as 'Joe Pea'. It's his son that's there now, John Rains. [Betty Dexter]

Chimney Cottage. Sweets.

You know where you go up on to the Flat? My grandma had a little shop there at Hillcrest [now Chimney Cottage], and, of course, when my dad died I was only a year old. We came to live down here, my mam and grandma, in this house here [now Mia Casa, West Bank]. Grandma and my mum started the shop up. Eventually, then, my mum got the chance to have papers, so she became a newsagents. When she died I took over, in 1955, and it was about thirty years or more before I retired. There was all sorts - sweets, cigarettes, tobacco. [Betty Dexter]

Wyn Tor Cottage. Sweets.

Mrs Scriven used to have a little shop in her house, and she used to sell sweets, crisps. She had a sideboard, and she used to sell crisps, biscuits and sweets from the house, like a little shop. [Anne Walters]

Forge Cottage. Blacksmith.

There was a smithy nearly at top of East Bank, Ben White. I've taken horses up there myself, up to Ben White. I used to meet him when I was going to school. He used to live down at Darley Dale, poor old chap. Before he moved to Winster, to live on the Flat, he used to come from Darley Dale on a push bike and do his smithy work all day - all shoeing and all iron work. He were a good fellow, he were. There were none of this 'come tomorrow' in that day. He'd get it done straight away. He'd do anything as we wanted. [Tom Wigley]

Forge Cottage. Blacksmith.

Ben White lived in part of your house [Orchard Mine Cottage], but he had his forge up at Lorna's [Forge Cottage]. He mainly worked with horses. He was one of the last blacksmiths. Everybody used to make appointments and come. When I worked at Ogston Reservoir, Frank Wibberley, who lived down the road, used to bring picks for sharpening every night. He'd drop off one load and pick the others up. I came out of the army in 1956, so it would be 1956 to 1960. He did all those sort of things. [Roy Walters]

FARMING 2

Cattle market on East Bank.

The Wigleys move to Painter's Way Farm.

I was nineteen when we moved down here with my father and mother, Maude, Em, and Ruth. Frank, my brother, was living at Bonsall. There were a Mrs Rouse - 'course she's gone now years and years ago – and she said to me, 'You don't know where you're going, you know.' She didna like down here. I do remember her saying that. This wasn't the only farm down here. There was that place up back [Great Close]. When we come down here Fred Slater, he wanted to leave that place, and, of course, it gave the opportunity for us to have 'em both, which we did. That was in '31 or '32. Of course, cowsheds were a bit dilapidated. They were falling, and, of course, that shed got built across yonder to put milk cows in, you know. It was hand milking and milk churns. Horse and cart for taking milk up to meet milk wagon at top. [Tom Wigley]

Yellow winter cracks.

Do you know where Great Close is? There's a tree there, and I've never seen one before and I've never seen one since. It used to grow yellow winter cracks. They were like a yellow plum, and I've never seen any only there at Great Close - you know, like a damson and a black plum. They were like a cross but were yellow, and they used to make lovely jam. I can remember my mum getting them from there. [Bert Boam]

Great Close Orchard.

There's not much now. They've made a mess of it, but I used to like to see old house and old buildings. Now there's just nothing. Great big orchard there were to it. I think they made cider. Lads saw what I judge to be a cider press and also a cheese press chucked out, you know. Trade would go, whatever, and then it would be, 'Oh, that - chuck it'. Good cider press up there, you know, 'cause they'd have to make money any road they could make some. But that big orchard weren't planted just for themselves, you know. Orchard would be above an acre, and they were all cooking apples, and a lot of damsons. It used to take me a week to get damsons up there. Me dad, you know, he wouldna leave 'em. I remember once, he were going to Bakewell cattle market. I couldna go at that time. I were only lad who were working. He said, 'Lend me yer coat'. I said I wanted it. 'Course, he had it in finish! They used to get these damsons at that time – they called 'em strikes or pecks. I think it were strikes, 80 lb. At that time of day it were either a strike or a peck. Well, there'd be a wicker basket, and that's how we used to convert 'em at top o' lane and teck 'em to Bakewell. They went to Turner's at Bakewell. I think his shop used to be up King Street. I'm over-running me tale a bit now. I got me coat back, and he hadna tecken 'is bit o' money out o' inside pocket. And do you know what he'd drawn for 'em - he'd got little invoice as well? Three ha'ppence a pound! And I'd been up that soddin' ladder! It were no bloomin' joke, standing up there. You wouldn't get very rich on that. It were hard going at that time o' day. But I think we were happier. I'm sure we were. [Tom Wigley]

The Johnsons move to Stoop Farm.

When I was seven, nearly eight, we moved from Youlgreave to a moor farm called Gratton Moor Farm. My father had always really wanted to be his own boss, and we loved it. Although I was a little bit lonely at first, we got to really love it, and we didn't want to move, really. After two years my father gave notice in, because my mother had been taken very ill with a heart attack. My grandmother was taken very seriously ill and died just after we came to Winster, which was the next move. I myself had an appendicitis, which had an abscess on it, and we had a very bad snowstorm. If it had been just the very next day, they wouldn't have been able to have got me away to the hospital, because the farm was up eight fields from a by-road and the ambulance just wouldn't have been able to get. There were very, very high drifts. In fact, I had to stay a month and three days in the hospital, because they just couldn't get out from the farm to fetch me.

We absolutely loved the moor farm. There was so much space - hardly any trees on the farm - and you could see for miles. When we came to Winster to Stoop Farm, which was previously the Angel pub, with my mother being very ill, she couldn't sort things out quite as fast as she would have liked to have done. So we all just dossed down in one of the rooms overnight, the first night, because it was quite late by the time we'd got all the furniture here. The first impression, when the shutters were pulled back - because there were shutters which we'd never had before - was of a closing-in feeling, because we were now right in the midst of a village, and it just seemed as though the houses were falling in on us. But now I wouldn't swap it for anywhere else. I just love the village now.

If you went straight into the yard at Stoop Farm the door was on the left to the farmhouse, and just outside the door there used to be a flight of stone steps going in what was the clubroom of the pub when it was called Angel Inn. Just inside the door at the top of the steps there had been a little ticket office, and I remember that we loved to play there. And then you went out into the big clubroom, which, of course, being farmers, we used as a hay loft. That was the upstairs of what is now Angel Cottage. Down below there was the dairy, and then there was a little back room - I don't know what they used that for, but eventually, when we had the milking machine, the engine used to be there. Further down, still in the Angel Cottage, there was a four-standing for milk cows.

Right opposite what was the dairy and the cowshed was a big wall for the next-door neighbours. Then there was the stable, and at the side of that was another cowshed, which I think held eight. And above, of course, we used that for the haylofts. Opposite there, there were outside earth closets and a pig crew. Further down again on the left past someone else's garden was a big cart shed, which they now use for a garage.

Further again we went through the garden and into a field, where occasionally we put the cows if we were going out anywhere and we wanted to put them somewhere quickly, and that is now used for a recreation ground.

Normally we would bring the cows out on to the street, down the Main Street and up Wyntor Avenue. It wasn't Wyntor Avenue then. It was just a very nice little leafy lane, and at the bottom of the lane there were the fields to our farm.

Stoop Farm wasn't a good farm. It was a poor farm, really. To supplement the income, my dad went to the Mill Close Mine for a while. Eventually he found this fluorspar and barytes. The barytes was on our own land. The fluorspar was on Mr Ernest Heathcote's land, and dad paid so much a ton. And he started to sell the barytes and fluorspar, which helped. We then had a boy come and help

> *Winster Wisdom: 'I'd better be gettin' off.*
> *If I dunna go, I canna come again.'*

on the farm. When this boy left school we had him work for us. My dad did have casual workers on the caulk and fluorspar. It would often be men who would do a shift of their own somewhere, and then come and perhaps do a couple of hours, drawing perhaps five tons of mineral out ready for the lorry to come and fetch it. Barytes is called caulk, and I think it was used for damping down the gas or the coal dust in coal mines. It was also bought for making into paint. They made a lot of it into paint. [Amy Slater]

Cheese press at Stoop Farm.

There were two big presses up there. I've never seen 'em as big as that. I reckon previous to that day sometime they'd meck cheese there, because they were enormous big blocks, you know, big gritstone blocks, and let down wi' a big screw and a big handle, let down to press on cheese. They 've been moved now. In the place where they were, they've made another little house, further down yard. There weren't any other houses in that yard when we were there. That as they've converted into a house, we used it for a corn place. And then there used to be a big copper in it, you know, a built copper and fire underneath. It would be for washing their clothes, I'd guess. [Tom Wigley]

The manure heap.

At one time it was called Stoop Farm where the Angel is. Cows and everything used to go down the Street. You never see a cow now like we used to on the street. Just over my garden wall all the midden and that from the cows was dumped. No-one bothered. They'd go mad today, all the smell. [Mavis Corker]

Driving cows down Main Street.

'cows on Main Street'

I think I were a bit of a rum lad! And some of 'em keeps it up all their life, you know! The farm at the Angel [then Stoop Farm] was through that gateway in the yard there. We kept milk cows at that time. I think we could only tie about nineteen down there. It worna much of a place really, you know. That's why we left, because land were all scattered. Then you had to drive cows down Street, up and down Street. I've seen cows come out of that archway where big doors are, and, of course, some of 'em liked walking down causeway, you know - a lot of 'em did. You know how cattle is, they cock their tail up - they've got no manners, have they? All sorts of things. It didn't seem to upset people. In that time o' day they were different. They didna mind, you know, they understood, but it wouldna do now. You'd get shot, wouldn't you? Wouldna do today! Well, it wouldna be safe today, turning a lot o' cattle out there. [Tom Wigley]

Muck spreading.

We had the fields down below Stoop Farm. It was hard work, because in those days everything had to be done by hand. If they were muck spreading, the cart would drop a heap of manure in a pile and move on and drop another heap, leaving them to be forked over the field. Sometimes I took sandwiches down to the men. I always wondered why my husband seemed to waste a bit of his sandwiches. He explained to me, 'We're muck spreading. We can't wash our hands, so we have to hold the bread by the corner and bite round and throw the last bit away.' [Amy Slater]

Taking milk churns to Darley Station.

The house that's now called Angel Cottage, that was just a farm building then. They used to milk cows in there. Those buildings down the yard, they had all to do with farm. Heathcote used to farm there then. Tommy Heathcote his name was. He had to bring all his cows into Main Street. They used to have to come down School Lane, and there were a mere at side of road against Leacroft, and they used to have to take them morning and night to drink at this mere, at roadside. You see, that's the only water they'd got. Heathcotes used to have to go to Darley Station, meet the quarter-to-eight train, take their milk in churns. And there used to be Heathcotes, Dales and Foxlows up the Bank. There were three or four of them. They all used to set off to catch that quarter-to-eight train. That's how it used to be in them days, take it all in churns. [Bert Boam]

Milking routine.

Milking was about seven o'clock, I should think - not very early. Milking was twice, morning and five at night. You should really milk your cows every twelve hours, but there's not many farmers does. It should be five in the morning and five at night. To make sure, you'd have to get up at about four. [Granville Johnson]

Milking by candlelight.

I could go in a cowshed - and I've done it many and many a score time - when it's blown candle out. It were hard work in winter. Of course, there were milking stool and milk bucket. You used to hold milk bucket and sit on stool. I could do it in pitch dark, feel me road. Just think about it, a cow at back of you, with them great legs, by gum! Mind you, they were used to it. It would be no good if you tried to do it now. I know when we started with milking machine, that were rough job. They didna like that. You'd fix unit down in between two cows, put clusters on, and bloody old cow used stand staring at it, and all at once leg comes up and unit were out. Young 'uns wouldn't do it today. They'd say, 'I'm not gonna get kicked!' I've been kicked a time or two. I used to walk out of that shed on one leg many a time. [Tom Wigley]

Milk to your door.

The milk was all brought round, and the churns were taken down to the farmhouse. Mr Foxlow's was the nearest one to us. They came round with the yokes on and poured your milk into your jug at your door.

'there were milking stool and milk bucket'

They had to carry these heavy milk churns on their shoulders. [Eileen Crowder]

Milk delivery and the village news.

Mary Dale lived at Gable House, touching the Hall. They were farmers, and they had the farm on the Horsecroft, and they used to bring milk out at night in little cans, about four in that hand and two in that, only about pint cans. And they used to deliver the night's milk at night and the morning's milk in a morning. They used to do a lot of talking and tell you any news, and all that. And sometimes they would be coming round at ten o'clock and half past! Kitty Dale and Mary Dale, they did it for years like that. And John Isaac Greatorex, he lived near the Manor at Newholme, he used to have two or three cows, and daughter used to take milk out as well. [Bert Boam]

Building up Roper's Farm.

Gradually Eric's father bought a bit of land here and a bit of land there, and that's how the farm started. Eric was born in 1918 and he left school and went to help his father. They went through a very bad patch in the late twenties and early thirties. The Milk Marketing Board was formed about then – I don't know exactly, but I think it was about 1932 – and there used to be a chap who collected the milk and took it to the Sheffield and Ecclesall Dairy and various other places, such as Nestlé's Milk factory. Before that time the milk sometimes wasn't sold, and it had to be thrown away or given to the pigs, or something like that. [Margaret Tomlinson]

Slaughtering cows.

Stephen Rains at Winster, he used to kill for Blackwell's and for Butcher Boam. And they used to do the killing where the new cemetery is now. That used to be the slaughterhouse. In them days they didn't shoot the cow. They used to poleaxe it, and you had to be an expert to poleaxe it. It was like a pickaxe with a spike, and it were hollow. And he used to strike at it and it used to go right in its brain. And if it were a nasty cow, he used to get some of us lads sometimes, perhaps at school dinner time, and he'd happen say, 'Aye up, you two or three, will you just come on for five minutes and hold this 'ere cow while I down it?' He put this rope round cow's neck, and it went through a ring and over the door. He used to get us two or three lads holding rope, and then he struck with poleaxe. And down it used to go, like that! But he was an expert. He didn't use to have two strokes. He could always down them in one. There were no shooting. There weren't such a thing as these 'ere guns then. [Bert Boam]

Pig farming.

We had pigs down here. I used to have about four or five, probably six. They'd be a good thing now, pigs would. At that time o' day, if you made a fiver a piece for your young pigs at about eight week old, you'd a job to do that, you know, in that day. I remember once there were a large white sow - a real good 'un she were. I kept her a year or two, and she were having these young pigs. It'd be middle o' winter sometime. The wind were coming up from east. It were

A prize pig, c. 1923. Donald Greatorex (left), George Will Stone (later a butcher), Bill Stone (pig-killer and landlord of the Crown), Henry Witham (owner of the pig) and Frank Blackwell (butcher and sometime landlord of the Bowling Green). The pig weighed 42 stones.

terrible cold, you know, and we'd no room for her. I put her in a big hen box, and she started having these pigs. You know, when a young pig comes it goes round to teat right away. But it were too cold. It couldna. I were losing these little pigs. I were perished myself, and everybody had gone bed up there. It'd be one or two o'clock in morning. I didn't know what I were going to do with these pigs. I were going lose lot. Anyway, I fetched an old cardboard box, put little pigs in and I went put 'em in here. I'd got all these pigs in this box. I came running across and I got through door, and I had to slam door in old pig's face. I could feel her on me heels. I don't think I'd time to put box down, because there'd have been no door on't house, you know. So I had to take 'em back. I takes 'em all back, puts 'em down. Old pig follows me back. And I suddenly thought - I'd got an old sack cloth. And I chucked it right over box, and everything went right. It stopped east wind comin' in, you know, and she reared 'em. You can't do wi' 'em. They're boss. Her were very docile, you know. You'd get them that would run you out o' place.

Another time, I remember, at night time - they used to come in at night on their own and in a morning as soon as it were daylight they'd chuck door off - I went in pigsty to have a look. One missing. I didn't know what direction to go. I went everywhere. And I went about a mile down valley, and it worna on our land. There was an old building down there, and there her were with ten little 'uns. Of course, I had to leave her. I did try to move her, but, no, you couldna move her, you know. I left her there about three days, I think. [Tom Wigley]

Barns.

And another thing, as you go round countryside you never see a barn hardly that's looked after now. They're all tumbling down. At one time, in my younger day, every one of those barns was in use. And there was someone in the village as would have two or three cows, and they used to have to go there and milk the cows. And even myself, I've even gone down to a building right down at Dudwood, which is from Winster a good mile and half, and I'd been there and had to carry the milk up with yokes from a building down there. That was morning and night, every day, seven days a week. [Bert Boam]

Dereliction and bombs.

The farm behind [Great Close] slowly disintegrated. It disintegrated all time, because we didn't want buildings. Actually, I think the buildings were unsafe. Then, of course, that cowshed were built across yard there, and we didn't need it, you see. In fact, when war were on there were bombs dropped around. One time that door flew open and that were a bomb down Via Gellia somewhere, and that flew open. You could hear bits o' rumbles, and I used to go up and see whether sheds were all right on top o' cattle, probably about midnight, because it wouldn't be a nice thing, would it, for them pigs be stuck under that thing. But I've not made a fortune, I'll tell you, not yet! Takes a bit o' doing, doesn't it. I'm just waiting for that fortune, for that quid! [Tom Wigley]

Belland.

You know, we suffer with lead in stock. Terrible. Young things - lambs and calves - we can't do anything with them when they're like that. It's no good. We take 'em to knacker man. I think he chucks 'em in bin, you know. Skin would be worth a little bit o' summat, but probably not worth it to skin 'em. To take 'em costs you money today, it does. You're no better off. You can generally tell by its symptoms. As I find it, if a calf gets it, it'll spin, kick and all sorts of things. Now lamb, it seems to be like as though its limbs has gone. I've picked lambs up on back there and its just like as if their back's broke, you know. They just lie down and they canna do a thing. But we don't keep 'em that side long. Shove 'em up here, you know, get 'em up here on gritstone. If you leave 'em there a long time, they'll get belland. Actually, it's lead in the blood, isn't it? [Tom Wigley]

The 1940 winter.

I shall never forget it. There was a very big snow and terrible frost.

I'd got my clogs on and one of my tops on, but we weren't very rich and we couldn't afford much at the time. A piece of this ice went down back of my clog. It froze me boot - just like that - froze it to it! Well, I'd two choices: either go back about a field and a half or go forward and get to the factory. If I go back, I'd still got to do the job, so I went through about six fields and down. My foot was frozen all time. Well, if I drop I should die, because nobody would find you up there. I thought, 'I don't want to die!' I were only fifteen. So I had to keep going to deliver this forty gallon of milk - brought some groceries back. When I came back, I couldn't feel I'd any foot on where I'd got this ice down. My mother got two kettles of boiling water, two large kettles, and she poured it on it. I couldn't feel it - it was gone frozen. At any rate that did the trick eventually. Of course, some hot milk down me and then we were well away. [Granville Johnson]

'my mother got two kettles of boiling water'

The bitter winter of 1947.

It was terrible in winter just at that time, '47. That were a good 'un, that were. We managed to get up to the village, because we had horses then, you know. They can plough through a big snowdrift. Oh, it *were* bad then. I remember every morning I got outta bed, I look through window upstairs there, and it were still snowing.

I think it snowed about three days. Wellingtons were no good, you know. I remember we had bags round feet, and then it were that deep up fields it used to get in yer pockets - snow. I don't think we lost many animals, because we hadn't got as many then. We didn't run as many cattle then as we do now. We had cattle tied up at other farm up there, and that's when I used to use horse. Jump on its back and go up there, you see. [Tom Wigley]

Haymaking.

Making hay is supposed to be a heavy job, but it was nice and light and out in the fresh air - against shovelling barytes. With a rake you turned the hay over and kept going round until you got to the end of it. If the weather was good you only got to turn it once, when it was really hot. As a rule it had to have a day on it, then you turned it over, and a day on the other side. You could mostly get it on third day, and, if it were very dry, you could get it on second. When it got up to about eighty or ninety, you could nearly get it as you cut it. We must have had about twenty acre all together.

We did eighteen dray loads in the day. There were nine ton about half hundredweight a load of hay. That's a fairly big load when it's loose. With the same field the easiest way is to have two drays. As you're unloading one, you're filling other. I picked eighteen load off one day. I did it next year and all. You were ready for your supper by the time you'd finished! The thing I hated about farming is just that it was seven days a week. I really didn't hate farming or hard work - I worked pretty well. But it's only that you did seven days. [Granville Johnson]

Labouring.

Ay'd just left school. Ah wer farm labouring at Holly Bush. Ah went six year. Ah wer cowman first. We use look after cows an grind corn. Chap that wer drivin' tractors hayee left, an ah had teck over all tractor work then. Ah use go theer on a bike twice a day. A little tractor we'd got. Use t'ave go back on Sunday then when ee left, feeding cows an grinding corn an mucking out an doin'. Ah had 26 year dairn theer. Use put a breel o' beer up an do. One o' me cousins, Benny Elliott at Ible, ah use go up theer an 'elp him, on bikes - haymeck, bring calves out, tag calves wi' ear tag, purra tag in ther ear fer market, oh ah, go out an get hay, an hawk barrels in, an everythin'. Tractor drivin'. Dun sum 'ours o' tractor drivin'. We use do wi' one tractor, get off that one, stop that one, an start wi' other one. Ah use t'ave drive two 'cause ah wer only one chap theer, like. Ah 'ad drill corn and then, and roll it then. Use teck a bottle o' ale and 'ave it on tractors instead o' tea. Use to 'ave a drink o' that - drink, like, while ah wer ploughin'. Yer didn't use t'ave a lot, 'cause yer might get drunk. [Stan Heathcote]

Haystacks.

Another thing which a lot of people would like to know about, you go about the country today, but you never see a haystack anywhere. At one time wherever you went in the countryside there were loads and loads of haystacks everywhere. Me, myself, used to build three haystacks on Bonsall Moor, because in them days you hadn't got means to cart it a long way, so you had to make your haystacks in your field. And there was always, like, they call it a stack yard, and that's where you built your stack year after year. To get them off the ground you would put a bit of a staddle wood down - like an old piece of wood which weren't much good for anything, like - and then put your hay on. Otherwise, if you didn't do that you'd get the roughest of your hay and the poorest and just spread that down to start off with. You could go down and get rushes down against Clough Wood, and then you could thack your stack with these 'ere rushes. And if you hadn't got any rushes to thack your stack with, you always used old straw or something of that description, either old straw or wheat. There was not much barley grown in my day. It was nearly all wheat or oats, mostly oats, because oat straw is thinner. When the oats had been beaten out, that straw then was just right for thacking. You used to get nut sticks to keep the rushes or straw on the roof. 'Pegs', they used to call them. Yes, hazelnut sticks, and sharpen them, and bundle them up, and then use your twine to go from one peg to another. You didn't use to stick your pegs in like that [90°]. You used to have to come at a hangle like that [oblique], so that, when rain come down, it touched end of your peg and went off. If you went in the other way, it would rain straight into your hay.

When you used the hay, you used to have to cut it with your cutting knife in blocks. And you had to take a section out at a time and keep going round down to bottom, and you cut it in sections, you see - myself I'm talking about now. Just between me and you, when Herbert Land were working for me and we had us hay up at the Study [Bonsall], at first we used to have to cut it on the moor out of the stack. Then eventually, as years went by, we managed to get a tractor and bring it down here. Then we had us hay for the Study here. Well, I used to be the cutter and Herbert used to be the carrier. I were cutting with cutting knife and Herbert used to stick his fork in these big blocks and carry it into the fodder'us [fodder-house], you see. We used to have one day getting hay in on a Monday and another day on a Friday, and that used to last us, like, for feeding. All the cowhouses then used to have what they call a fodder'us, another part, like, where they used to store their hay to last a day or two, so they could go in the fodder and just put it over the cows. [Bert Boam]

Oats, grains and turnips.

In my younger day I had this farm up towards where you go to Matlock, right against Salters' Lane. I've grown wheat, barley and oats up there. They used to put them up in sheaves, and they built them round so all the ears went in the centre. You used to keep the middle stacked up more so, if rain did get in, it would run off. We used to bring them off the moor and down to the Study [Farm, Bonsall], where my buildings were, and there was a person from Elton who had a thrashing machine who would thrash the oats. Baileys from Matlock brought your cattle nuts and feed for your milk cows. They'd bring your cattle feed, take your oats or wheat back, roll or grind them - whichever you preferred - and bring them back the next time they came, when they brought the cattle feed. Then, in wintertime, we used to have grains - what they made beer out of, like hops - and put them in a pit and cover it over and try to make it airtight. That's how they kept. We used to go to Bakewell Market and buy a load of turnips, and they'd bring and tip them up for you, and you used to have to pulp your turnips and mix the oats and grains with the turnip as a feed for your cows. You never heard the word 'silo' in those days - there weren't any. [Bert Boam]

Wild birds and animals.

That's another thing I was going to tell you. When I used to go to school - I can remember as if it were just today – corncreke [corncrake] every year used to come. Where the houses are built now down the school way, there on what they call the Leacroft, a corncreke come there every year. And it made such a noise, this corncreke did. It's, like, rather a big bird, and there used to be mostly two of them. I don't know if the hen made a noise, but the cock bird used to make such a noise. It *were* a loud noise! I've never heard a corncreke since I left school, and I've never seen one. So all them things have gone. Same as skylarks, you could be up on the moor and you could see, not one or two, you could see as many as a dozen soaring up at different times. And they don't half make a lovely noise, whistle lovely! Now I never see one. And the cuckoo, it was nothing to hear several cuckoos round about, everywhere. This year I've never heard one, and I've not heard of anyone else hearing cuckoo this year. Once I heard a nightingale. That was when we came off work. They started two shifts on the surface once at Mill Close, and it was six in a morning until four in an afternoon and the other shift was four in an afternoon until two o'clock in the morning. Funny hour to knock off, weren't it? About half a dozen of us were coming off the surface, not underground, and it were about two o'clock in the morning, and we were coming through Clough Wood. And somebody said, 'Hey, listen at that.' We all stood there. And it were the nightingale, and it were marvellous, and I've never heard a nightingale since.

Oh, there used to be ever such a lot of animals about at one time. Hares up on the moor, and that, there used to be quite a lot. I've seen as many as six hares in one field, but now I've not seen any. As things go about they come with fertilisers and have different methods and so on, and it does away with things then. At one time nearly every farmer that had got cows - even those that had only got two or three - they'd have some from a farmer who'd got a lot of turnips, or something like that. They'd buy a bit of a load off him. And at one time there were ever such a lot of turnips that were fed to cattle, and most farmers used to grow turnips. Now, no one ever grows 'em, not a farmer. They don't feed turnips to cattle now. There used to be a lot of partridges come in field then,

Winster Wisdom: 'The only thing you can't use from a pig is his squeal.'

because they could hide under turnip leaves, these partridges could, and they'd survive like that. Now turnip fields have gone, partridges have gone. It's same with such a lot of things. They've killed these insects, and a bird that lives on them insects – the insects are no longer there so the birds aren't there - and this is what keeps happening. [Bert Boam]

Asa Cooper remembers farming as it was.

I didn't really choose to come to Winster. I was just, off-hand, looking for a house. I'd lived with my in-laws for six months after we'd got married, and I went to pick up a Matlock Mercury newspaper and saw this house at the top of Winster Bank for sale, and I came to look at it and bought it. I started farming from there. I didn't have any intention of farming when I first came. There was no land or anything with the property, but after a short while some land came for sale. When I bought my house I sold everything I'd got to buy my house with, and then I had to start from scratch again. I bought a cow and reared calves on it, and then when they got to about twelve months, sold them to buy a couple of fields of land and a small building. Probably carried on and did the same thing for another twelve months and then sold them again and bought a bit more land and went on with it. It was 1967 when I first came to Winster, 21st November. That was the same day that my daughter Gill was born.

Round '67 a big farmer would perhaps be milking around about 30 cows. Slater's have always been biggish farmers, at Whiteholmes Farm. Mr Horace Johnson's down in the village here, they milked probably 20 to 30 cattle. He was a biggish farmer because he had, I think, two sons working at home. The majority of farmers milked 8 or 10 cattle, or maybe 12. Ted Dale would milk probably 8 or 9 cattle, then probably keep 5 or 6 young beasts. Everything in them days was done with horse and carts, which was a slow job. Ted Dale farmed from Horsecroft, by the bottom of West Bank. If you started to cart a load of manure from Ted Dale's farm up on't top of Shothouse, it'd probably only have two small heaps on a trailer and take half a day. He'd probably have to go by New Road with it. It'd take him half a day to take a load. Then he'd probably have to call in at a stone barn and bring himself a load of loose hay back for cattle for the next day. Hand milking, you see. It was a good man that could milk, probably say, four or five cows in an hour. So it'd probably take two hours to do t'milking. By the time you'd got them out again and cleaned out and fetched the fodder in for t'day, it was time to start again. Bert Bateman farmed up on Back Lane, that small building there, which tied down 5 cows. It's called the Limestone Way now. Mr Bert Bateman, he was a roadman, and did this, like, as a spare part-time job. Mrs Hope was his daughter. He farmed and grazed on the Headlands as well. You see, in olden days farmers used to graze the roadsides with their cattle and on the Common. Farmers used to have the rights to graze that common land. I can remember that in my time. Sam Foxlow, he farmed up Pikehall Lane. When I knew him he lived up Woolley's Yard. It was a different Sam Foxlow from the one who lived on East Bank. He milked in that barn up there, and I think it was in 1958 when we had such a rough, bad gale that it blew his cowshed down, flattened his shed, and I think he gave in then, like. He retired. And all those small farms up there - Bill Bateman and Bert Bateman and Sam Foxlow - they all had to bring their cows to that watering hole to drink water, at Mosey Mere. It was a self-made pond on its own, and they would keep it clean because they relied on it for water for their cattle. Bill Bateman's land still has its sheds at the bottom of Bonsall Moor Lane. His son Ewan uses that land. Joe Walker was at Bank Top Farm, the one we call the Poor House now. Joe used to work at t'quarry and farm in a small way down near the school somewhere, in them little barns down there, and then Bank Top came up for sale. It was sold in the Miners' Standard pub one night. He gave about £4,000 - about 76 acres. They didn't spend a lot. Whatever they made - if they got half a crown, like - it was saved. He said he couldn't pay for it all at once. He once told me it didn't take him long before he could pay for it. He worked hard. I don't know whether Kate had a bit of help from where she worked. She was out in service for Mr Ernest Heathcote down there, and I think she was left this property up Woolley's Yard and probably some plots of land by Mr Heathcote, for her services. I don't reckon it was a particularly good thing at the time. At that time old property was a liability. You couldn't sell it. In fact, if you tried to rent it out to somebody at probably only a few shillings a week, they'd probably want more repairs doing than what the rent came to. So, you see, old property in them days, it was a liability to own it. She had, I think, quite a few of the houses in Woolley's Yard, about seven cottages that she'd left to her, but I think that she'd probably have looked at it as a millstone round her neck rather than a decent legacy.

I gradually built up my farm just by rearing calves, rearing a few sheep and lambs, a few pigs. Living very tight [Asa laughs], not spending, wasting money. And it sort of grew from there. I started with one cow. Then I kept rearing calves and that type of thing. I never milked myself. I've always reared beef cattle. I've probably milked a cow and then suckled calves with milk from it. I started milking when I was about four. Used to milk about five cows before I went to school. There was definitely a knack to milking. The routine a dairy farmer had to follow was just a seven-days-a-week, fourteen-times-a-week, milking-twice-a-day routine - a lot of hard work for very little money. But a lot of farmers were fortunate to have farms handed down to them from their parents, and they'd got no rent or anything to pay, so they had a better chance of making a living. There were other jobs round the farm, of course. Sheds had to be cleaned out twice a day, fodder had to be got in, turnips had to be pulped. That's hard work, but when you're young you don't think nowt of it, do you? As you get older it takes more doing. Hay was all got loose, you know, with horse and drays. Days semt be longer, weather semt be better in them times, and hay'd always be got in. There was a Mr Bryan who lived in Winster. He'd go out contracting to farmers, mowing fields with a scythe. He said a good man can mow an acre in about two days, for probably a few shillings. I think he said he used to mow that field up Pikehall Lane, which is about an acre, for about eight shillings. It all had to be turned with rakes and forks by hand and then loaded on to drays and made into a stack. And the stacks had to be thatched to keep t'weather out of 'em.

Farmers grew their own crops. They grew mangels, turnips, cabbage, kale. They grew oats, which was cut by a binder and made into sheaves, and then it would be thrashed and get the grain out of it - roll the oats, feed the straw or bed the cattle with the straw. They were more self-sufficient in them days. Kept less stock and produced all their own produce. We don't grow mangels any more. Labour costs, you see. If somebody wants £4 an hour now to go into t'field, thinning mangels or pulling mangels and topping 'em, it'd cost a fortune, wouldn't it? They're similar to turnips, but a bit more like a big sugar beet or fodder beet. It were a good feed and kept cattle and everything healthy. They were very healthy when they ate a lot of greens like that, you know, cabbage.

Because I only had a few cattle, I suppose I did get sentimental about them. Everybody did in those days. A good cow would be kept from anywhere from 12 to 14 years, and probably have 10 or 12 calves, which now-a-days they bang through, and they only last 3 or 4 or 5 years a cow now, with this mechanism they've got. The change-over from cattle to sheep rearing started, I think, when milk had to go into pipelines, then into steel vacuum bulk tanker things, and then the small farmer couldn't afford that sort of thing. So they packed up milk producing and then produced a bit of beef and rearing calves. Then they started with a few sheep to mix in. In the 1930s the Milk Board took over and bought your milk. But then that was when it was carted to the dairies in 10- or 12-gallon milk churns. In olden days, before my time, it were 17-gallon milk churns, but I don't remember handling them. Then it all went to be collected by bulk in tanks instead of churns. So it put a lot of small farmers out of business. In order to make your farm acceptable to the government you'd have to build a new milk shed, buy a new tank, put a pipeline in, refrigerators to freeze milk, because there was no fixed time of day when they'd probably collect it. Churns used to be cooled by water - an old refrigerated cooler. But a lot of old-fashioned farmers didn't go for that sort of thing. It was too expensive to work, too hard for the money they'd got. Plus now farms have got that big, farmers are now probably milking 300 to 400 cows. One big farm nowadays takes the place of perhaps twenty small farmers.

I've always had sheep since I were about sixteen. I've had sheep for 45 to 50 years. They were a lot cheaper to buy in them days. You didn't make as much difference on your lambs, but you was better off than you are now. Up to this last couple or three years, if you went to buy a good young sheep in for breeding, you'd look to make anywhere from £80 to £200, so you were making £40 on your lamb. You were still no better off when you were giving £5 for a sheep and making £7 a lamb in 1960s. Only thing you've got is there's a lot more money involved in it, in't it? Losses get bigger. It's definitely hard work! I don't know that I felt it was harder then. I were younger then, and it weren't harder then than it is now - for me, anyway. Last holiday I had were when I got married, 33 years ago. Went to Scotland for honeymoon for 14 days. That's last day's holiday I've had. Wife goes away, but I don't. I don't think retirement will ever happen. While we can keep going, I think I will do. I reckon I'll die on the job, so to speak. Probably find me dead in a field somewhere! [Asa Cooper]

Laying pipes on East Bank.

Breaking roadstone.

Granddad Boam's job was breaking stone. I can remember - although I mustn't have been more than five years old [1914] - but I can remember granddad giving me a hammer, like, sometimes on a Saturday or something like that, or perhaps I wasn't old enough to go to school. He used to get a piece of rock and put a bag on and give you this hammer and let you break stone. You used to break stone for the road then. There was no tarmac. They used to sell it. Granddad used to, sort of, pile it from here to there, and he had like a cane, a yard, a stick, and he used to measure this way and that way. He used to taper them up somehow, build them up, like, and then it used to look ever so lovely. They were wider in the bottom and they used to come up a bit and were as flat as a pancake on top. And they used to measure the depth there - a yard that road and so many that road - and sell it to the Council like that. I'll tell you where the old quarry was: where Winster reservoir is now, coming down the West Bank. Now it's grown over, but that's where granddad's quarry was. Granddad's quarry was all rock, but it's all grassed over now. Then I think they used it as a tip. They used to tip ashes and everything when granddad had axed stone out of it. So it's, like, been filled in again, roughly. There used to be a lot of ashes, tins and all sorts in them days, and they all used to be tipped there when granddad had the stone.

They used to put the stone on the road, and then they used to put limestone dust. And they used to have a water cart and wash all the dust into the limestone. There was always a steamroller in those days, and the steamroller bloke always used to have a caravan parked somewhere, and he'd live in the caravan - not in a house. As years went by and I got to be about nine or ten years, me and Cyril Wagstaff on a Sunday when we came out of the choir - because in those days you were made to go to church - we used to go to the steamroller bloke into his caravan and think it was lovely. He parked his caravan wherever they were working. If they were working going up Pikehall Lane, he'd park it some- where at the side of the road, somewhere where it was handy, and so at week- ends you could go there because they used to live in it. It was like going to their home. [Bert Boam]

'there was always a steamroller in those days'

Quarrying.

It was more or less like quarrying, as you might say, when you were using a hack and shovel and you were hacking your stuff down ready for shovelling, more like quarrying. You'd hack and shovel all day on to the lorry. I got £3 a week and my food, and that was working for barytes. It's better known as caulk.

It goes for making face powder. Face powder is made out of barytes, crushed, and lipstick that's made out of red oxide. It was what the old miner had thrown away. We'd get it on at Brookdale, just on the suburbs of Winster. It's only about half a mile away. [Granville Johnson]

Spar mining.

Ah went up to Long Rake then. Ah 'ad a crushin' job fer abaht five years, an then I wer tapping lead out o' diggers. Then ah wer tipping fer a while. Thee tayed me off that. Ah held record for 130 a day up shaft in wagons. Ah've got record upstairs o' what ah tipped. Thee took me off that. Ah wer mecking too much money! Ah wer on bonus, yer see, an thee wondered ... we got so much bonus.

Then thee 'ad me on bagging. Ah bagged 22 ton one day meysen from behin' a waggon, coat up in air. When ah cum teck me shoes off and 'ave a wesh at naight spar cum out of. Use cum in ere an – wait – oh, that's a lump o' hard spar. Use sheck yer feet, if yer hadna got any slippers on, yer'd cut yer feet. Many a piece o' lead ... put it in back place like. Oh aye. Ee wer up theer 26 year, an I wer up theer 23, an ee got that presentation clock.

I were feedin' spar inter crushes be hand. Manager cum up one day - hay went o'er Middleton mine - an he says, 'Can yer throw a bit faster?' Elevator wer poor, yer know. Frank said, 'It'll brake in ayf. That'll cure 'im.' So he oppened up two or three minutes an' broke elevator down. 'Ad stop for a wick then while we repaired it. Ah put twenty-five ton through in one day, ah did, be hand, feedin' it inter crusher. Aye, when ah wer fit. Ah wer on me own, under a shed, tippin' it all wi' digger, screenin' roun' back, an bringing it ter mey pu' through. It use be 'ard work in them days. We use start at twenty ter aight til abaht quarter ter five a' naight, aye. Yeh, clockin anyb'dy on an thee didna show up. Sumb'dy clock sumb'dy on an thee didna show up an thee got peed! [Stan Heathcote]

Accident down Mill Close Mine.

What made me move to Winster was I'd only been married a month when my husband broke his leg, you see, working in Mill Close Mine. He went down and the cage hit him. So they took him down to hospital. The two Dr Fletchers were down at Darley Hospital at a meeting, and they sent him home with a great cage to put over his leg. They came the following morning to see to his plaster, and they left all their plaster fingers on the end of the bed, and it all dried on, and it ruined it. And it were a new bed. We'd had all new furniture from Eyre's. Do you know, we furnished two bedrooms and living place and kitchen for just under £100, and I've got the bill upstairs. And the rent was 5s 6d a week. Anyway, Michael had broken his leg, and he was off work nine month. He got compensation, £2 a week. It was like sick pay money that he paid into a club. Their money always used to pay into a club - the Foresters, I think. [Gladys Hardy]

Pumps at Mill Close Mine.

My husband was an engineer on the pumps at Mill Close lead mine. If one of the pumps wasn't working, it made the other two more to do. He had to get it repaired quickly. There were three pumps: the large one was called Jumbo, the second one was Alice, and the small one was called Baby. [Dolly Brassington]

A miner's snap.

He came home and said these boys had thrown their sandwiches at mine wall, where lead had come from. They were that fed up with them - bread and jam again - and they just swat 'em at wall. They said they'd go hungry sooner than have them. You'd have thought they'd have changed it, because a man doesn't want same thing every day, does he? I'll say this much, it's a problem what to give them. There's cheese and meat and mixtures and I don't know what. I'll tell you what he did used to like: pork dripping. And you *could* get a piece of pork them days! I know one time my mum came see us, and they went in Oxley's bus. And she found she'd picked parcel up off of table and taken Bill's snap with her! He should have had it for his dinner. Any road, *she* took it instead! [Gladys Hardy]

Chimney sweeping.

Mr Hope up ere he wanted his chimney swaypin'. He cum ee said, 'Cuz sweep Tom Wigley's chimney?' Ah said, 'When were it last swept?' 'Oh,' ee said, 'It's not bin dun fer ages.' Course, when ah went dairn wi' chimney sweep tackle, theer wer that much soot an it cum dairn like thunder. Yer couldna see in hows. Ah said to Tom, 'How long as this bin like this?' Ee said, 'Oh it's bin a good while in chimney.' We wer humping it out in wheelbarrow, gerring soot out.

'it cum dairn like thunder'

We swept it, an I don't think it's ever bin swept since. Ah started spitting black up. Ah wer dooin a fertnit wi' spitting black stuff up off me stomach. Ah said to Tom, 'I dunna feel very well after sweeping tha' chimney, ah dunna. Dunna teck me dairn theer agen.'

A day or two after - they'd got a Rayburn in, sem as we'd gorrin ere - he said 'We've gorra leak. All watter's coming thro' ceiling up above. All 'ot watter cums dripping dairn.' He said, 'It'd scald yer if it hit yer a' back o' neck, y'know. One o' lads has 'ad t'use tha' insulation tape. It wanted a new fittin'.' So ah said, 'Ah've gorra teck that Rayburn out.' Ah said, 'What's it held in place now?' Ee said, 'Yer could gi' ah a nudge out wi'it.' So ah gi'im a nudge out, an put him summit else in, like. [Stan Heathcote]

Apprentice wheelwright.

When I left school at fourteen I was an apprentice wheelwright. You know Square and Compass at Darley Bridge? The landlord he had a wheelwright business adjacent to the pub. They've altered it all now, but there used to be workshops at the side. I think it's bed and breakfast now. They've made it into holiday cottages. I should have gone in the army when I was eighteen, but in them days the war was over. Your employer applied and you could get deferred until you were twenty-one, until you finished your apprenticeship. So I stayed there until I was twenty-one. My first wage was 12s 6d a week. [Les Bacon]

Thacking stacks.

Shaw his name were, and he lived next to Gildings. His trade was thacking stacks, what they call thacking. He used to go down to the Clough Wood and cut all these bulrushes - any time there were rushes - and bundle them up. People in them days, they had to make haystacks in the field. When your stack were built and your roof, well, he used to put all them on the top, same as what they do a thacked house. That was his trade. [Bert Boam]

Slacking lime.

We used to fill up our buckets from Roy's house side. That was the tap where we all filled up. At the bottom of your garden [Orchard Mine Cottage] when I was young we had a big lime pit under some stone. There were a big hole there in the corner where you jump over the wall if you want to go down the field. We used to fill up from that tap, because we used to slack lime. Bert Boam said when I was a little boy I used to sit on those steps, covered in ants, selling lime for a penny. It was a penny, and a ha'penny extra if I coloured it. We used to have the lumps of lime brought in from the quarry down the Via Gellia as you're going up to Brassington on your left, Ben Bennett's. They tipped it on the road, and my dad and Uncle John they slacked - it's called slacking - in a big metal container, and it was poured out into a sieve over a barrel into this deep pit in your garden. In two days it was slack, like thick cream. And people used to come with big milk buckets - and they'd still got the ladle in - and some people with little buckets. In my later career as a decorator I was doing three or four pantries every spring cleaning time with lime. Yes, these old houses had lovely pantries. We coloured it with dried powder, and it wouldn't come off your hands. They used to say, 'You and your lime!' [Harold Barnsley]

> *Winster Wisdom: 'Don't do all your work today –*
> *there's all tomorrow not touched yet.'*

Pay and conditions.

When I were only about four year old [1913], my father worked at the old Mill Close Mine - not the one that drowned, the one before - and they only got paid every seven weeks, which was a £1 a week, they used to get. So they used to get £7 in seven week. All your bills for groceries or anything, you had to leave them until my father got his wage at the seven weeks' end. When somebody was off work and didn't have any money, people in the shops just gave you a bit more credit in them days. You could run it on, like, especially the villages. You knew one another, and there were so many people related to one another. Now there's a lot of strangers come in, but at one time there wasn't a stranger entered the village. They were all relations, and one used to help one another. Even myself, when I had the milk round, there were just one or two in the village, like, and they were very bad payers, and they would run and say, 'Well, I'll try give it next week.' And it would keep going on till it got a long while, and then you'd have to write that off, really, when it all finished up, in some cases. But you seemed to manage, you know.

In my time you used to get six shillings off the dole, but you had to walk to Matlock, either from Winster or from Bonsall, or anywhere. Same as anyone working at Masson Mill, or anything like that, if they were on the dole, they got six shillings a week in them days. Most days you could see some poor old man walking from Winster to Bakewell, and they'd call on the roadside somewhere and get a can of tea. They used to have just a tin, like a fruit tin, just an ordinary tin, and beg for a can of tea, on the roadside. But they used to have to walk from that doss'ouse at Bakewell to that at Ashbourne. You could see them walking there, no toes in their shoes, worn away. It were a long way to walk from Ashbourne to Bakewell.

Another thing, as years went by a lot of people that worked at Mill Close lead mine used to walk, all weathers, right from Middleton-by-Wirksworth to Mill Close Mine, and work a forty-eight-hour week, six day week, for £2 17s in old money, if you was a labourer. But if you was a machine man, you know, drilling or anything, you got £3. So that was £150 a year. But they walked all weathers, right from Middleton and places round that to Mill Close Mine, did their work, and then had to walk all that way back. And there weren't any grumble then. Now they get all these big hand-outs. It was ever so poor, you know. Anyone that was ill or anything, like, it was marvellous if they got enough food to live on, really.

There used to be the Friendly Societies, but you used to just pay half copper or two, and it wasn't much, like. You used to get very little out, only a matter of a few shillings. There was one called the Oddfellows and other called Foresters, and they used to keep the flag and that at the Bowling Green, in the club room. They had parades. I forget what time of the year, but there'd be one and, a while after, there'd be other one, just parade up the street with a band in front of them. And it *were* a big occasion! And some of them used to have a scarf round them - a Foresters one. [Bert Boam]

Death of a casual.

Muggins was a casual, one that used to come very often. And he always came near the harvest to help with the harvest and haymaking or corn harvest later on. He'd been a time or two. He had a sister that lived down at Darley. And this Muggins came Friday night, and he went into the blacksmith's shed into the far corner, as it might have been. And the blacksmith always left his shoeing box there. When I went out on the Saturday morning I went up to Ben's gate and had a look, and he was sat on this box, stretched out. And I said to him, 'Aren't you very well, Mr Muggins?' And he said, 'No'. I took him a mug of tea. I didn't know if he'd got anything to eat, I never thought to ask. I didn't bother any more, because I went down to my mother-in-law and stopped for the day. When I came back he was stretched out, dead. So, of course, I thought my best plan was for bobby, policeman, see what happens. I didn't, sort of, know any more then, but they came and took him away. The next thing that I had was a letter from his sister thanking me for doing for him, the one that lived down at Darley, opposite St Elphin's School. [Gladys Hardy]

Village doctor.

Doctors worked different hours, because you could. There was nobody to tell you what to do. You made your own rules and regulations. If you said you were going to have Thursdays off, everybody would know that you were going to be off on Thursday. One of the doctors would be there in an emergency, but you'd know you wouldn't go for your medicine on Thursday or for a weekly dressing, because that was doctor's half day. They didn't all have the same half-day. We had Thursdays, and we went to the theatre in Nottingham, just went anywhere, disappeared. We used to go to a lot of local things. I've been abandoned at dances. I've been abandoned at dinners. Sometimes I've never even noticed. Desmond would go and I hadn't even realised he'd been away and missing for half an hour.

When Dr Stoker came here, people paid for the health services out of their own pocket. You charged wealthy people as much as you dare, and let the poor people off with as little as you dare. That's how it worked, really. Sometimes it meant that poor people didn't come as soon as they should. But he was very soft-hearted. He'd know more or less whether they could afford it or not, because you get very poor-looking people and they're probably quite wealthy - miners you know. He generally knew what was going on and he charged accordingly. [Marjorie Stoker]

Getting to work.

I went to the village school and left at fourteen. I helped my mother for a while, but I got fed up of this. I went off to Matlock one day and got a job at Paton and Baldwin's, a wool factory - angora wool, rabbits and goats, but originally it was more or less goats. I did various things and worked my way up. For a long while I was on the office staff. I reckoned nothing to biking, because you had to push your bike up Wensley. I had a bike, but I reckoned nothing to it. There were such a lot worked there, and Masson Mill. There were such a lot biking in those days to these two mills - girls - but some of us used to walk to Darley Station and get on the train. It was only a few coppers return. We caught a train at Darley Station about quarter-to-eight, and were up at work at eight o'clock. Charlie Ashton, he was a clerk on the railway at Derby, and he used to catch this train every morning, so we knew there was going to be one man on the road, even when it was dark mornings. We knew there was going to be Charlie. But we always wanted to be in front of him, because he walked very fast and we knew we'd be on time if we were in front. There was a person who lived at Darley Bridge, whose name was Iris Pepper. We picked her up on the way. She was so slim. I've never seen anyone walk like her, but I kept up with her. I was determined to keep up with her. If you kept up with Iris you'd definitely get there for eight o'clock. That was before the buses started running. When the buses started running they were workmen's returns. You got a bus to work, and during the war it took us right there. It was a munitions factory during the war. [Mildred Witham]

Working in a cotton mill.

I worked in Arkwright's Cotton Mill in Cromford. I went started sweeping up. We had to until we were about fourteen. Then, of course, if you showed any initiative for your work on this bobbin winding, you were alright. Then I went on to cop winding, then tube winding. Then it went from us up into the sixth floor for reeling, to make into yarn, and then it went back to Manchester. The men were working in the doubling, because it were too dangerous down there for any woman. I remember I had a cousin named Lillie Fern, and she'd got longish hair. And she was down doing one day, and it snatched her hair and pulled some of her scalp off. I was there from thirteen until I was twenty-three and I were married. I was there ten years. [Gladys Hardy]

A working life, 1927-80.

I left school at fourteen and went to work at a public house in Youlgreave called the Bull's Head. The odd jobs were sweeping the yard, looking after the pigs, and cleaning people's shoes that were on holiday. The pay was 5s a week and two meals. Being from a poorish family, my father thought it was not much, so we'll try and get him in somewhere else. So they got me in at a spar mine working for 10s a week at the Middleton Mining Company at the top end of Youlgreave (also known as 'Bacon's Mine' as most of the workers were called Bacon). I was taking a lot of food, because I had to walk nearly up to Parsley Hay where this mine was, which is a good four mile. I used to take a shoebox full of food, and by the time I got there I was ready to eat it. Of course, dinnertime wasn't until twelve o'clock. When they came to have dinner the foreman sat in a little cabin and would say, 'Right, let's have a look what you've got today.' And he'd pick my shoebox up and show it all round the cabin. I don't know how many slices there were but this shoebox was full, and a bottle of cold tea. I'd been there about a fortnight and I got a rise from 10s to 10s 1d. That carried on for a short while. At the same time as I was there the Prince of Wales was riding in the Flagg Races, and from the bins that I was working in at this mine I could just see the horses at Flagg.

Well, that wasn't very good, 10s 1d, and I was eating more than what I was getting, so they got me in at Friden Brick Works. I travelled on the Silver Service bus, and the fare for the week was four shillings. But my father found he could buy a bike for 3s 8d a week, so that's how I got my first bike - £4 17s 6d. The first week there I got paid 37s 4d. Times were a bit hard and we got put on short time. I went on the dole and I was only getting 5s a week off the dole. I hadn't been at Friden long before my father died. I was only fifteen. Three months later my mother died, and that left me looking for lodgings. I went into lodgings along with my brother – he was paying 25s a week, and she was charging me 15s because I was only a boy. This went on for a short while and then she rose this board to £1. Now then, I was on the dole at different times and only getting 5s, so I couldn't afford the £1 very well, and I had to scrimp and save. One day we got arguing and I, sort of, fell out with her and left. I came to live with my sister and brother-in-law for a short while, but it was a long way to cycle all the way to Friden. It was hard going if I went up by Miners' Standard and over the top. It was still hard way if I went through Youlgreave. So I went to lodge with an old lady back in Youlgreave, and I stayed there until I got married in 1939 and went into the army.

I started work at Friden again after I came out of the army. I did two years there, and with being in the army I'd been broad-minded and learnt a little bit more about things, and I wasn't satisfied with what I was getting at Friden. So I went and asked the manager if I could have a little bit more. He got his slide rule out and said he didn't think he could give me any more. So a friend of mine said, 'Why don't you come down to Enthoven's? He said it was alright down there, and for every shift they give us a spare man, and the spare man does nothing. I thought that was handy. I'd been making seven thousand bricks a day at Friden. I give my notice in and went to Enthoven's, and the first job I got was what they call 'Coal and Ashes'. That was fetching coals for the pot fires and cleaning the ashes up that had been fetched out of them. Well, I could do that in about half-an-hour, but it lasted 'em all day. I had nothing to do then. A bit different from Friden, where we stood at a press for eight-and-a-half hours without moving. I was there from about 1948 to 1961 and I got a little touch of lead poisoning, so I decided to leave and went back to Friden for two years. Money was a little bit better then, but it was shift work. Stayed there two years and then Magnesium opened up. That's near Wirksworth. I was there with them for three year and they shut down, so I was made redundant. But it didn't take me long to find another job. I went to the Battery at Bakewell and worked for them for three-and-a-half years, and then they closed down, making me redundant a second time. From there I went to a firm of Italians in the name of Guillini, and they set up a mineral plant doing fluorspar. After three years they shut down, so it was a third redundancy for me, and a pay-off of just £450.

I was getting pretty old by then. I was sixty years of age, so it was getting a bit hard to find a job. I tried one or two places. Down at the Dole Office they were sending me to places that weren't suitable for me, not at that age, carrying hot bitumen in buckets to different places, roofs and one thing and another, which was very heavy. In one of the quarries, handling bags of lime dust - that was another heavy job. Anyway, I went to Enthoven's, saw the manager there, and he said, 'Let me see, if I'm thinking right, you're as old as me. You're too old for this place.' On the way down the yard I ran into one of the day foremen: 'When are you starting?' I said, 'I'm not starting, nothing doing'. A bit further down the yard I saw another shift man: 'Are you starting a' Monday?' 'No', I said, 'Nothing doing'. 'Right, I'll go and see him'. I started on the Monday. They set me on. I stayed there until I came retiring age. I asked the manager if I could stay on because, with being made redundant, I had no work's pension to fall back on, so I worked a bit extra to get a little bit more money. I stayed on for another eighteen months, and that were it. I retired and settled down to do bits of odd jobs, gardening and mowing the churchyard, keeping the grass down in the cemetery. [Bill Slaney]

Bert Boam remembers his working life.

I've done a lot of jobs. When I left school I wasn't thirteen years old [1921], and I got a job with a man named Heath, and he had a man working with him who used to cart coal from Darley Dale Station to Winster. But the horse could only pull 10 cwt up Wensley, and he used to do two journeys a day. He'd go about eight o'clock in the morning and land up in Winster sometime around dinner, and then he'd go and do another load in the afternoon. Well, I got this job with Heath, because the man who was working for him was going to leave and go to Mill Close lead mine. My job was doing his job, fetching a load of coal in a morning and one in an afternoon with the horse and cart. I wasn't thirteen years old, and it was just near Christmas time. So the first morning I took the horse and cart down to Darley Station, loaded 10 cwt of coal on the cart, but the roads were just one block of ice. There wasn't tarmac. The roads were all made of limestone. I was coming up Wensley, just past Oker, when the horse went down. I had to sit on its head and keep shouting, 'Help!' A man eventually came and he got some coal out of the cart to put under the wheel to stop it. We managed to get some of the harness unhooked off the shafts and get the horse up, and, as luck would have it, it didn't break any of the shafts. I had to leave the cart and bring the horse as best I could on the footpath up Wensley to Mrs Heath, and I told her what had happened. She said, 'Well, you'll have to take it up to Vincent's and have frost nails in.' They used to be great big sharp studs. Mr Vincent was the Blacksmith up the West Bank at Winster. He used to shod horses. There were always horses all day long stood waiting to be shod. Mrs Heath then said, 'I'm sorry, but I don't think you can have the job now. I don't think you're old enough.' So I lost the job.

Cauldwells, the butchers, were right against the Market House in Winster. The shop itself was facing up the street towards Elton, but it was joined on to

Bert Boam, 1998, aged 89 years,
outside Orchard Mine Cottage, East Bank.

the house. It's now a garage. Cauldwells were butchers and farmers. In those days there were so many small buildings. There was one up Woolley's Yard, and now it's a bungalow, but that's where Cauldwells used to go milking. It used to be the British Legion. There was another one near the Rock Field, and I think that barn is still there today, on the other side of the road on the Common. Another one, they call it up the Headlands where the toilets are today, Cauldwells used to milk several cows up there. Another place was a few yards up East Bank, where there's an archway on the right-hand side. As you went under the archway to the back there were some buildings there, and Cauldwells had milk cows there. So you had several places in Winster to go to. When you went milking you had to carry your milk back with yokes and cans. When you'd got different places like that it used to take you a long while, because you had to go and milk the cows and clean them out, and so on. So I went to work for Cauldwells. There were two more men working for Cauldwells. One was Arnold Greatorex, and he helped me to learn milking. So I used to do what I could - clean out, help to feed and help to carry the milk back with yokes, because there was more than one person could do. I was only just nearly thirteen, about 1921.

I was only with Cauldwells about four to five months. You used to have your breakfast, dinner, tea and supper with them, because, when you were farming, days were never finished. You'd be working until nine o'clock at night, and you had started about half-past-six in the morning. But you never bothered about finishing time, because you had your cows to milk. I got no money, just the food, and they used to call it 'a good table'. Different people cook different, and Cauldwells were noted for good food, and they were butchers.

I went from there to Oddo Hall. I just happened to get this job. Garretts wanted a gardener, a handyman, and dad used to go at the weekend and do bits at Garrett's. So when they wanted someone permanent dad got me a job. Well, they were gentry, and they had three servants and a cook. But it wasn't the same as Oddo is now. It was just like a castle. You could go up this tower - that was if Mr Garrett allowed you - and there was always a big flag on top. You could see all over Stanton Moor. When I was there Mary Slater was the cook. If you did an errand for any of the servants or the cook, they used to make a fuss of you, and when you came back you'd have either a fancy cake or something like that. And you thought the world of that. It was such a good job there. I earned 12s a week, and they used to shout you in about a quarter-to-twelve for your dinner, so I had dinner and 12s a week, which was really good. I just used to have to go at weekends, same as on a Sunday, to see to the greenhouse, and so on. I worked about twelve months at Oddo Hall, but they pulled it down. There was nothing wrong, only they had to have three servants and a cook, it was so big. Turner was the name of the people who bought it, from Sheffield. They were ever so well off. They used to have knives - had a factory at Sheffield - and she was a lovely person. They pulled it down to make it more easy, and all as she had was someone to look after the little girl, like a nanny. May Worthy, who lived at Bonsall, she used to work there looking after the little girl.

My brother, Randolph, he was working at Berricliffe Quarry in the blacksmith's shop, and whilst I was up at Oddo Mr and Mrs Garrett died. Eventually I had to have another job. My brother went out on the hearth, which was more money - that was making these gritstones, great big circle things, using the pick. That was very good money, but if it was wet time you didn't get paid. It might be wet for three or four days one week, and you'd be wet through. You used to put a bag round you until your bag was soaked through, and then you couldn't work any more. So when you went in the cabin your time was knocked off. Some weeks you'd only come home with 10s or 15s. So I got my brother's job in the blacksmith's, and my brother taught me blacksmithing before he went on the hearth.

As time goes by they started two shifts at Mill Close Mine. A man came and said to my mum, 'Aye up, we're starting two shifts at Mill Close Mine, and it's a good wage - a guinea a week to start.' You were picking stone off a sort of table that shook, like riddling, and you were there to pick all the rough stone with no lead on and chuck it down a chute. All the rest went on to be crushed. I would be about fifteen years old, about 1924. They started two shifts on the surface, not underground, and the shifts were ever so strange. You went on at six in the morning until four in the afternoon, and four in the afternoon until two the next morning.

So I was at Mill Close, and everybody who worked on the surface, there was one big building where you had your snap in. There was only a brick wall divided it from the boss' office, and when a new person started they used to do tricks in them days, like get this 'ere belt paste and put it on his private parts. Well, this new man was George Stone. He was a Winster lad and he was a big strong lad, and me and Charlie Gratton got him on the floor, and he was sprottling and squealing. And suddenly, right in the door place, stood the boss. He said, 'Oy, this is how you do it, is it?' So he said, 'You'd better come for your cards.' So me and Charlie got the sack. He said, 'Do you know, Boam, I'm ever so sorry to part with you, I've watched you through the window and I've seen you taking barrow loads of lead across for some of the men. You seem a good worker, but I'm sorry I can't do any other only sack you. But I'll tell you what I'll do. Your brother has been down to me this morning. He wants a job.' It was my brother, Harold, who lives at Matlock now, and he'd been there for a job, but, of course, there wasn't a job then. But the boss said, 'Now you can go home and tell him to start in the morning.' So that is how my brother got the job at Mill Close Mine.

I didn't know what to tell my dad, but he said, 'Oh ne'er mind. You're all right. What's-his-name, he'll just do with you.' Dad worked for Tommy Twyford at the gritstone quarry at Birchover, and he said I was just the right bloke for him. So I went, and dad said to Tommy Twyford, 'Now this is him.' And he asked me if I liked a bit of farming, and I said, 'Anything.' He said, 'Some days you'll be at quarry 'ere, and some days you'll be at Hawley's Bridge at my brothers' farm. So this Twyford who owned the quarry at Birchover, he had two brothers who owned the farm at Hartle Hall. For the first day or so I used to go in the house at the farm and have my dinner with two of the Twyford brothers. One was married and the other wasn't married. After about a week or so I went and had my dinner and not thinking I lit a cigarette up, and I didn't ask if it was alright. The next week when I went there the servant said, 'Oh, you're not coming in for your dinner. I'm going to bring it you in the stable.' One of their children, he was only about three or four, and he said, 'Can I come and sit on yer knee, mister, while you have yer dinner?' He sat at the side and we got talking, and he said, 'You're not coming in our house no more, mister, for your dinner, because you smoke.' So I never went in that house no more for my dinners. Actually, I ought to have asked, but I didn't think, because I could smoke anywhere else and nobody would say anything. Most of my friends smoked, and always Woodbines. I've been smoking Woodbines ever since I used to go milking down Dudwood with Bert Mosley. He always used to give me about half a cig, like, and he started me smoking.

Winster Wisdom: 'That that is nowt is never in danger.'

There was one that was called Abe Twyford and the other was called Ralph, and they had a bull. Abe Twyford was left-handed and he used to have a short piece of wood, and when he let the bull out he used to say, 'Now get at the back, clear out', and you'd have to go at the back of the building door out of the way. But this particular day Abe had got this piece of wood and the bull tossed his head a bit and Abe struck at it, like, with the stick. And then the bull went for Abe a bit with its head down and Abe struck it again with the stick, and it gored him to death in the yard.

Another thing happened. When I was at Bakewell, they were round the ring where they were selling cattle, but up that part it just happened that at that moment there was hardly anybody about. The drover used to have a lump on his head. He was getting on a bit, in his sixties, and he'd got a stick. And this bull - it seemed funny because it hadn't got horns - and yet it got him somehow and chucked him as clean as anything straight over, and he went 'bash' all in the cow muck, and he *did* go a thump on his head. I shouted, and a lot of people came from round the ring, and the bull went a bit further up, and some men managed to get it in one of the pens. A chap gave me a £1 note and told me to fetch a mug of brandy and I ran to the pub for this brandy and a chap said, 'Would you run to the police station and get an ambulance?' The ambulance took the injured man away, and about three weeks after he died. He looked just like a shuttlecock. You've never seen any human being fly through the air the same as he did.

At Hartle Hall there was a man by the name of Gregory who was the head deputy, and he lived in Winster. You used to have three deputies on each shift underground at Mill Close. Kenny Gregory, who lived up West Bank right against the Burton Institute, was the head deputy on one shift. For some reason he took a liking to me, and he often said to me - when you've finished work and you gather at top o' street and talk an' that - he often used to say to me 'Aye up, lad, why don't you come down mine? It's a regular wage down there. At quarry some o'time you're not getting much money, are yer?' I said that, if it was a wet day, I'll agree. He said that down the mine I'd get £3 a week every week, whether it rains, hails or shines. Although I thought I didn't want to go underground, it had been a bad week and he'd seen me at the top of the street. When he asked me about going down I said I'd been at the quarry since seven o'clock that morning, but I'd come off at five o'clock and have my tea and then go down Mill Close Mine the same day for ten o'clock on Gregory's shift. I was the youngest down the mine. I was just sixteen.

I stopped there until the water came in. The water came in when I'd been there about a year, and it drowned out, like. Have you ever seen any of the books about 'The Mine that Drowned'?

Instead of going on the dole, which was 6s a week, I went out farming. I went out service to Oats - you know, where Shothouse Spout is, that farm opposite. In those days there used to be a horseman, a cowman, and so on. Ernest Roskilly, who lived in Winster, he was the horseman, so I went as cowman, and Bernard Bunting, who lived in Bonsall, he was pigs and hens. Oats had about thirty-six

'I stopped there until the water came in'

milkers, and when there was a cow calving I had to stop up for the cow calving, but you didn't get more money. And you used to get such good meals - breakfast, dinner, tea and supper - when you were out service, living in there.

So I lived in there for just over a year, and then they got the steam pump going and the electricity and they managed to beat the water at Mill Close. They started setting a lot of men on. It was three shifts and there were such a lot of men working there then. We used to go 70 fathom down, and walk three quarters of a mile. The loco used to run on the main run and it got to a certain point. So, wherever men were working, they used to bring all their wagons with the lead to this point, and the loco used to take them to the shaft and draw them up.

I got with a man named Joe Vardy from Darley Bridge. There were six of us on a shift, and we were sinking another shaft because they had found lead down further still. I was the shot firer. I've still got the certificate to say I can use explosives. When you were going to fire your shots you used to have a piece of wood like a rake handle and a piece across the top with two nails in, and you used to stick your fuses in there to keep it out of the water. Your ladders were steel and they were permanent - fastened into the rock side. This particular day I'd been up for something, and I was talking to a chap called Reg Young, and he was on the winch. He used to use a lever for the compressed air to draw the bucket up when you'd filled it with stone. We were just going to fire the shots. We had our fuses fixed up ready and I was going down to Joe. I was at the top, and my feet slipped off the top rung. It was these steel clippets that were on my clogs. I tippled backwards, and the first thought that came into my head was I thought I would be dead in a second, and that was as much as I knew. They found out after that I hit this wooden plank with a pump on, and that broke my fall a bit. And then there was about two foot of water, and they reckon that with me hitting that and dropping in the water I managed to survive. I was black and blue, but I didn't break anything. The drop was 40 foot. Joe Vardy was there, and he kept saying, 'Oh dear, lad, a thought tha' were dead! Oh dear, lad, a thought tha' were dead!' The deputy came and got me out of there. I was in bed for a while. There were no sick pay, I never got a bean.

Can you see across Black Rocks to that house? Every time I look across, this memory flashes back. There were six of us on one run and six on the other, and we were on that run where you put your wagon under the chute and filled it and then you took it down to a collection point. The other six brought them from the bottom of the shaft there, and brought their empties to fill - so you had two sixes. Amongst my six was a lad in the name of Bert Lomas. This house you've been looking at, there was a chap in the name of Byard, and he was one of them sort, 'I'm 'im, I'm frightened of nobody,' and he wasn't very well liked, and he was on the other run. This particular day he brought a wagon up and he threw it off of the rails and into the water. The water was 18 inches high, and, when you used to then get your wagon, it would be all full of water and it took some pulling back. I said, 'Hey, what's going off?' He said, 'Next un that comes up is goin' be same.' I said it was dangerous, so, of course, when they went with their wagons my other five mates said, 'Are you goin' 'ave a go at 'im?' I said, 'Ah flippin' am.' They knew very well as I'd have a go at him. He comes up with the wagon and he throws it over again, so I thought, 'Right, me and you are for it now.' Can you picture it? I went in, left, right, left, right, and he slunk right down in the water and he yelled out. They got hold of him and they had to take him out and he had to go home. Somebody fetched the deputy, and they let me stay until ten o'clock, and then the deputy said, 'Now, tomorrow you can't come down the mine. You'll have to go and see Mr Williams.' I had to go and see Mr Williams and I had to explain to him. He said, 'I'll leave it over for a couple of days, and we'll have to fathom out what's what.' This Byard sent word that he was going to take me to court. Mr Williams said they didn't want any court case, and said the best thing for me was if I went and paid Byard a fortnight's wages, which was £6. He said he was going to sack me now, and I was to come round the other way and come up the stairs and he'd set me on again. That was Williams, the head man of the mine. Well, I was palling about with a lad at the time by the name of George Waller, and he had a motorbike and I had a motorbike. That Sunday night, me and George, we had to go up to Byard's, right against Black Rocks, and I had to knock on the door and the missus came. She invited me in, but, when she said it was me, Byard said, 'If I'd a known it were you, you'd not 'ave come in.' I asked him if he was going to take it to court, and he said he was and that he was getting compensation. I said I'd pay him a fortnight's wages, £6, and he could either accept that or take it to court. Anyway, he accepted the £6, so I had to go and see Williams and tell him he'd accepted the £6. About a fortnight later Byard came back, but Williams said, 'No more, you're finished 'ere,' and sacked him, and he never came to the mine again. When it all boiled down, Bert Lomas had said something about this Byard, and that was why he's caused the trouble. This is what it was all about - he'd got the wrong Bert. I was still living in Winster at that time and would have been about twenty something.

Eventually, I was palling about with another lad called Jim Baker, and they were wanting shot firers at ICI at Buxton, and it was good money - more than 1s 6d an hour, a lot more money than you got at Mill Close Mine. So I said to Jim about going up to Buxton, but Jim was only an ordinary wagoner, whereas I was a shot firer and I had a certificate. So I went up and got this job, because I had this motorbike. But we had to sign a paper that we would lodge out in Buxton, because they wouldn't allow us to travel. When it came to, Jim ran in, but I'd given my notice in at the mine so I thought I'd go on my own.

I was courting at the time, and we had come out for a walk, and who should we run into but the chap who lives across the road there, Sammy Elliott, and he had six lorries and was wanting a driver, but lorry drivers weren't two-a-penny then. I could drive. I started at Gilding's in my spare time and at weekends on just a tonner, and I did go on different lorries for anybody if they were ill, just for a day. I learned like that, and then dad bought a new car from Stockport, and if you had a new car they gave you two hours to show you how to drive. Hilda, who I was courting, didn't want me to go to Buxton, so she said to Mr Elliott that she'd heard he wanted a lorry driver, and he said 'Aye, can your bloke drive?' When she said 'yes' he told us there was a long-wheeled Bedford in the garage, key would be in, and, if I wanted the job, to go there at half-past-seven, take it down to the East Midlands Electricity Board at the back of the cinema at Matlock, their headquarters, and they would fix me for the day. That was it. I had two jobs then. I had either Sammy Elliott's job or this Buxton job. I said to mum I didn't know what to do in the morning, whether to go to Buxton or whether to go to Bonsall. Buxton was a lot more money than Sammy Elliott's, but I'd got to live out at Buxton, so you had to weigh one thing against another. I sat on my motorbike at the top of Winster Bank, and I didn't know whether to go to Buxton or go to Bonsall. Finally, with courting Hilda, I decided to come to Bonsall.

Some days you'd be on the Electric and some days you'd have to be slack carting from Matlock Bath to Masson Mill, and they used to expect 24 ton in eight hours. You'd nearly sweat blood. It used to be trickling down you. It was a rum job. If you didn't empty that truck, they used to have to pay demurrage on them. For every day it was stood after that first day they used to have to pay a lump sum of money on it, so they wanted that truck emptied. You could only get three ton on the lorry, that's all it would hold - choose how you piled it, it couldn't hold any more. You used to have to go from there to Masson Mill on to the weighing machine, weigh it and tip it up by hand. Twenty-four ton by hand in eight hours and it took some doing. I used to try to get a load landed to Masson Mill at dinnertime, twelve o'clock, so Hilda could see me out of the room. And then she used to come and have her dinner with me. About nine or ten o'clock I used to put a brush on the roof of the truck so that she could see. If she saw the brush she knew I was slack carting that day. So she used to come out and have her dinner with me in the cab. And then we got married in 1939, when I was thirty, and that's when I left Winster and went to live in Bonsall. [Bert Boam]

Dr Fletcher and his walking stick.

I remember old Dr Fletcher. He was a real character. I always remember he used to knock on people's doors with his walking stick - to save him hurting his fingers, I suppose. [Marion Drinkall]

Two Dr Fletchers.

In the Dower House there was a Dr John Fletcher - mind, I was only very young then, so I can't tell you a lot about him - and Dr James Fletcher lived up West Bank [at Bank House]. They were two brothers, but Dr John was retired and Dr James was in practice. [Betty Dexter]

A death from pneumonia.

My father, Paul Thomas, was married twice. The first time he married a lady called Elizabeth, who died in tragic circumstances. She'd got three children, two girls and a boy. The boy was four years old, and the girls, I think, were seven and ten. Elizabeth had a cold, but she said she was alright. She had a bad night. My father, her husband, worked at Mill Close Mine as an engineer, and he was doing some important maintenance at that time on one of the pumps. So he had to go off to work, and she said she'd be alright, she'd get the children to school. Then her illness, the cold, turned to 'flu, and from 'flu to pneumonia. She had her sisters with her – there were four girls all together – and they didn't know what to do about it. They could tell that she was very poorly and they ought to send for the doctor, but they daren't do it, because in those days the doctor had to have the money before he came out (this was Dr Fletcher from Winster). It was common practice in those days, because people generally were very poor and couldn't pay doctors' bills. They decided they'd have to go to the mine and get his permission to send the money which they had in a box on the mantel-piece. It was supposed to be for the children's illness, not for the grown-ups'. Anyway, they saw someone at the mine dressed up, who they took to be the mine manager, and asked him to get a message to ask Paul Thomas to come home immediately, as his wife was seriously ill. Whether or not the manager passed the message over, nobody ever found out. Paul never got the message down the mine. His work would have been difficult to leave, because the pump had got to be in service before they could leave the job. Anyway, when he got home about eleven o'clock that night he found her in a very poor state with pneumonia. She was gasping. He ran all the way to Winster to Dr Fletcher's, taking the money with him, and helped the doctor to get the horse and the cart, lamps lit, etc. They came back as fast as they could, but as soon as Dr Fletcher saw her, he said, 'No.' But he tried hard. Her family had been using the family bran bags, apparently the only known method of reviving anybody with pneumonia, but they'd only been putting them on the front of her chest. The back was just as important as the front to get to the lungs. Anyhow, she passed away in the early hours of the morning. Afterwards Paul married Elizabeth's sister, Mary, who was my mother. [Harold Thomas]

When Aunt Florrie had twins.

When Dr Stoker first came he used to take children's tonsils out up there in his house. He was a surgeon. His wife used to help him. She was a qualified nurse, you see. Before Stoker, there used to be two Dr Fletchers. There was James, that had the surgery in Bank House on West Bank, and Dr John at the Green Gates - that's called the Dower House now. We paid when we went to the doctor. When my Aunt Florrie had twins - they didn't know there were two babies, you see, in that day - they only prepared for one. The midwife sent for the doctor, and Dr James Fletcher went down to deliver this baby – to help the nurse with the baby, because she was at home, of course – and there was something wrong. So he sent for Dr John at the top of the street, and Dr John said, 'There's another baby, that's what the matter is.' A boy and a girl she had. Say a mine shut and there was a family and they didn't have a lot of money, they paid the doctor's bill over a period of time. I think the doctors were very lenient in that day. [Mildred Witham]

A moment of fame.

Dr Stoker was our doctor. He came and said, 'Betty, come outside and stand at the door. I want to take a photo of you for this book.' So I went. At one carnival they had an exhibition in the church, and there were all sorts - everything you could think of, old things and modern things. And there was all his different photos of Winster. And, of course, he'd got this one with me, and it said, like, that Mrs Greatorex took over the news agency from her mother who'd died. So I was famous! [Betty Dexter]

'A bob's worth o' buns.'

There were a baker. That was just down a yard or two, down Pump Lane, on your left - Mr Boden. It *was* good bread! I've fetched many a shilling's worth o' buns from there. They were grand, you know. I do remember when we come from Kniveton to Winster, me and my dad, he'd got horse with a load of furniture in dray, and I were behind him with another horse with a harvest implement. Well, we landed home to Angel, pulled into yard, and I do remember him saying, 'Go and fetch a bob's worth o' buns.' It's funny how you remember these bits of things. And it were a big bag full, you know, in that day. [Tom Wigley]

Baker Boden.

My parents had a bakery business in Bank Road, Matlock, established in 1903, and from there they moved up to Winster in 1913 to Pump Lane. A Mr William Wild, that owned all the property there, his sister used to live next door to mum and dad down Bank Road, and he pleaded with my father to go up to Winster to the premises there and start up the bakery business. He said if my father would only consent to go he would let him have the business premises for a whole year without any rent. So, of course, after much heart-thought they did move up to Winster in 1913. They just opened up what was one of the front rooms, and they had two counters that they took up with them from Bank Road and the fittings. Anybody casually from Winster used to go in to buy the bread, because I understand there was already another baker up East Bank. My father, meanwhile, kept on his rounds in Matlock and Matlock Bath and all round there. As they saw the horse and cart going down, people in Wensley would come out and ask for bread. That eventually started up a round down Wensley and round Oker. In Winster people gradually kept coming for their bread and their buns - he was noted for his bun loaves.

My Uncle Abel at Youlgreave, he had a round around Elton, Birchover and Stanton, and they came to an agreement that my father should have the Elton round. So he went on deliveries twice a week - Tuesdays and Fridays - up to Elton. From there it gradually got that the farmers wanted him to go all round Grange Mill, Pikehall, Longcliffe, Aldwark, and all round there, so that was quite a big round. That's how the business grew, because he was really a first-class baker. He was very noted for his home-made pork pies, all hand-risen. They would come from all round at Christmas time. He'd be a whole week baking these pies and the bun loaves and the sugar buns - anybody would tell you about that. Even in those days people would come out from Sheffield on Saturdays to take back so many loaves and so many of these bun loaves. It was good, home-made, first class, because he always had the first-class flour from Bailey's at Matlock, and he was noted for his brown wholemeal bread. Any of the neighbours up at Winster will tell you that. And that's how it grew.

My mum helped in the bakery. She was a real right-hand. I was born March 29th 1914, and I understand it was a fortnight after the hotcross buns, because he had very famous hotcross buns. There I was, a fortnight old, while all these hotcross buns were being made. So I was absolutely brought up in the business. [Bessie Thorpe]

Winster's many Boams.

The funny part about it is that there were so many Boams in Winster. There was Butcher Boam, and he had two sons. They were different Boams from us. There was Stanley Boam and Cyril, two sons belonging to the butcher. Then there were last house at the bottom of Pump Lane on the left. There was another Boam lived there, who was not related to us or Butcher Boam. Then again there was Herbert Boam, and he lived up the Bank, near where there's a footpath and you go through the Headlands. None of them were related, either. [Bert Boam]

A large family.

Going back to the old days, about the forties or something like that, there was another well known family, the Coopers. They were a local farming community.

They had rather a large family – fifteen or sixteen children, I'm not sure. But in the 1947 winter, I can remember them coming down into Winster village to the local bakery to collect their week's supply of bread in milk churns. They used to pull sledges. They tied the milk churns on the sledges and pulled them back home. But the thing that sticks in my memory is the father turning round to his eldest son and saying, 'Asa, 'ave we gorrum all yet? Can we go?' There were so many, he didn't know how many had gone down with him! [Derek Wood]

Toby Thorpe.

Walter Thorpe was brother of Sidney Thorpe, the schoolteacher, and Robert Thorpe, the shopkeeper. He was in the Special Police. During the war he used to go round the village watching out for anybody who'd got a glimmer of a light. It had to be absolutely blacked out. I always remember, he went to Joe Rains, and Joe's doorstep was a little bit worn, so consequently a bit of light came through. He said to Joe, knocking on the door, 'Joe, you've got a light here.' So Joe says, "Ave I, Toby?' (They called him that because that was his nickname.) He said, 'Yes.' He said, 'Well, I'll tell thee what, Toby, when they come round in submarines I'll black it out.' He liked to show authority, did Toby. He was only about five foot. One year Ray was sledging down the Bank, and, not being able to stop, he got ravelled up under Toby's cape. He couldn't get out, and, of course, Toby wasn't very pleased about it. The cape reached to the ground, and, with Toby being so small, he looked just like a little bat. He was a nice man. He used to come in the Bowling Green when we kept it. One day they were talking about shoes and feet, and he said to this lady, 'I bet I can get your shoes on.' She said, 'I don't think you can, they're only a size three.' But he did, he got the shoes on, so you can tell how small he was. [Dot Fearn]

'Lift me in and I'll drive home.'

Toby Thorpe used to live in Ephraim House on East Bank. He was a very small man. He was an air-raid warden once. People said that, because he was small, he used to try to show his authority, but whether that's the truth I don't know, because I was just a child. He had a charabanc and he used to take the men to different football matches, cricket matches or such things, and they would all call at the pub and be there for quite a while. And Toby would have as much as any other - this is only hearsay - and he would say, 'Lift me in and I'll drive home!' I don't know how they never managed to avoid an accident. [Amy Slater]

Miss Smith and her cakes.

If anybody wanted any cakes, Miss Smith would always bake some. I know my mum, with being busy making up in the pork shop, Miss Smith used to make us a dozen cakes every weekend. She lived at The Old House on East Bank. She used to take in the lady schoolteachers as lodgers. They stayed during the week and would probably go home at weekends. [Dot Fearn]

Mr Hodgkinson and his flowers.

Mr Hodgkinson lived with his mum on the Croft, where Keith Wright lives now [Tatra Mount]. He had a big garden, and he used to sell six pennyworth of flowers to anybody that wanted them. [Dot Fearn]

Henry and Sylvia Bark.

Mrs Bark lived directly across from the Bowling Green, and she used to make oatcakes. Her husband never worked, only just to sweep the occasional chimney. Even then she used to carry the things for him. Mind, he wasn't a well man really. He wasn't a robust man at all. [Dot Fearn]

Toddy [Tommy Todd] and Harold Durden.

They say Toddy was in the Police Force, and he had to come out for some reason, I don't know why. So he worked with Fengels, when Fengel owned the Manor. He lived in the offices above. Well, when the Manor was sold, old Toddy had nowhere to live, so Mr Stone, who kept the Crown, offered him a room. It was like a loft. You had to go up some wooden steps up to it. He was a lovely character. He was from Sunderland. Annie, my friend, Mrs Slaney, used to do their washing on a Monday night, and I used to go up and give her a hand. Toddy would be there doing the mangling, and we had some real laughs with him. He was a smashing man. There were one or two characters, but my favourite of all was Harold Durden. Now Harold looked after old people for as long as I can remember, and he lived with Miss Durden and Billy Durden. When they died he lived with the two Miss Rains, who lived at the Archway. They were rather eccentric old people, who liked a drop of whisky. Old Harold used to cook and look after them. Anyway, when they died he

Dot Fearn, 1998, aged 74 years, on her usual seat outside Stanfree House, Main Street.

was left without a home, so he went to live on Anson Row, the cottage at the end. Harold was the local bookie, and he used to have a little basket in which to collect his bets. The miners who were going to work would drop bets into his basket. I remember one particular day - it was Grand National day. He often called and had a bit of lunch with me - he was ever such a lovely old man. And he said, 'There'll be all these women backing horses today, Dot. I can't do with 'em when they win.' He said, 'They never back all year round, and on Grand National day they come up with a winner.' He said, 'I'll bring my bets up and you can help me to sort out.' Well, I listened to the race on the wireless, and it was a horse called Sheila's Cottage that won. Harold came in and his face was absolute raging. He said, 'What did I tell yer! All these damned women 'ave backed Sheila's Cottage, thre'pence each way. Never see 'em all year round!' You see, it was a woman's name and they probably knew somebody called Sheila. Anyway, we sorted it out, but it's a wonder he weren't bankrupt. He was marvellous in his day. He was a pianist. My mum bought me this piano from Matlock - it was £15, and that was a lot of money in them days. Harold used to come at four o'clock every day. 'C'mon, get practising,' he'd say. He knew the theory but his hands were a bit stiff and he couldn't manipulate. Anyway, he'd probably stop and have his tea with us. I should never be able to play if it wasn't for Harold. He knew immediately when I'd hit a wrong note. [Dot Fearn]

Joe 'Pea' Rains.

I was talking to John Rains last Saturday. I pulled up and got talking to him and asked him how long he'd been living at Winster. He told me he was born in Winster, and who he was. 'Joe Pea' they used to call his dad. He used to have a little flat cart, a white pony, and take his greengroceries round in that, because in those days you didn't go shopping. Everything used to come to your door, even your meat. Butchers always brought your meat round on a Saturday. Joe Pea played the squeezebox for the Morris Dancers. [Bert Boam]

The man who picked up a donkey.

Wilfred Boam, lived in the Main Street, and he worked at Mill Close Mine. He had a brother, Herbert - and he was a great big massive bloke, he were. He once picked donkey up, instead of taking donkey round and through gate. He got hold of donkey, picked it up, and put it over wall. Once he was footballing at Miners' Standard - that's in my younger day - and he was the goalkeeper. And something went wrong, so he went and grabbed hold of referee and he got his hands round his neck and he held him up in air, like that! [Bert Boam]

Arthur and Polly Heathcote.

Arthur was always smiling, and he always wore grey flannel trousers with a

> Winster Wisdom: 'If his brains were dynamite,
> they wouldna blow his hat off.'

brown jacket. When he went down the street he always raised his hat to every woman he met, and always, when I were a young lad, I used to nip round the corner just to catch him and say, 'Good morning, Mr Heathcote'. And he would raise his hat and give me half-a-crown. Always. And he used to get us apples, windfall apples, for years and years and years. Mrs Bince did the same when she was here. They brought us apples and things. That's a good while ago. Mrs Marsden never brought us any, 'cos she was a queer suss, she was. Mr Heathcote, he always had us to sing Auld Lang Syne on New Year's Eve. We had to do Auld Lang Syne round here and be shouting and merry.

The gate on the end of the path at Heathcote House, Arthur Heathcote had a tennis court there, you know, and entertained his guests there. I've seen Princes from Birchover come here in their horse and trap in the early '40s. I was only a young child then, running about, and there was this great big horse int' yard. And a car came down and this horse shied and it lifted that cheese press. There was a hook in it, and it lifted it straight up and dropped it down, and it never hit horse. Then Arthur decided he wanted some hens, so he ripped tennis court down and sold it, all mesh and wire and all bits they'd got. And then he had some hens, and many a time he had to go and rescue Polly out of the hen box. The cockerel kept flying at her and pecking her on back of neck, and it also did my mate Dale. He was telling me about it the other day. A mutant brute it was! It flew at you and pecked anything. Dogs wouldn't go near the hens. It flew at them. Looking after his own, you see, because he thought it was an enemy coming. Polly went to collect the eggs from the box. She got int' box, and he had to go with a cane. He'd attack Polly int' box getting eggs, you see. He wouldn't let her take eggs. When Arthur died they carted the boxes away. I remember them going, and Stones at the farm took it over, the tennis field, the garage and the lot, you see. [John Millward]

Sam Heathcote and the Derbyshire dialect.

Well, Sam Heathcote, he'd struck all his matches and he couldn't light his pipe, because they were damp. There were two hikers in the pub, sat nearby, and so Sam says, 'I dunna suppose any on yers got any on yer?' He meant, had any of them got any matches on them? And they couldn't understand him. So I said to them, 'In other words have you got a match to light Sam's pipe?' They still say things like 'sithee', instead of 'see you', until they're stopped by the teachers. And 'sirrah', instead of 'sir', was a word used ever so recently. They still say, 'Ey up, sirrah!' - that's another one. [Dot Fearn]

Eric Shimwell.

Eric Shimwell was a character on his own, and he could relate back to way before when I was a child. He used to tell stories about my childhood that I'd actually forgot. He did bring up on one occasion my twenty-first birthday party, which was being held at the Miners' Standard. It was an open house, everybody invited. Unfortunately, I was out at work - it being a family business - and I rolled back at half-past-nine at night, and went into the pub midway through my party, which had been on-going since seven o'clock. My father turned round and said, 'Oh, you're back. I thought you'd be back about now.' He said, 'What does it feel like to be a man?' I said, 'I'll tell you when I'm drawing a man's wages!', which Eric thought was rather amusing, and started to clap. [Derek Wood]

Tony Longden.

Tony Longden, a miner, was involved in the spar industry, as far as I can remember. I don't know what mining he'd done previously, but he was a character, he was, and he could relate stories back to when the Mill Close Mine was working. Very often they'd get a gang together and they'd sit at a table and they'd be relating all their old memories. He used to tell

Stan Heathcote (left) stops to chat with Stan Hope on the Flat, East Bank, 1998.

the story about when Mill Close Mine was flooded and closed. They were characters on their own, but we didn't get involved too much in the conversations, because it was in the middle of our work - keeping the pub in Winster Hall. Our work was their pleasure. [Derek Wood]

Some Winster characters.

Anyway, we'll start from bottom of Street, nearest Wensley. There were Johnny Wild. He was an antique man, he were. He could get you sofas, a rocking chair, anything you wanted, old Wild could. He'd get you owt you wanted. Then there were John Isaac Greatorex at Newholme. He were a farmer and he lived there for years. He used to have a spittoon, and he could spit straight into the spittoon. He were a crack shot at spitting. There were Stanley Boam, and he used to put candles and light 'em ont' wall, and Stanley could whip the wick off with his bull whip and not cut the candles - take the flame off of every one, six in a row. The bull whip were about 30 feet long. He killed pigs in the slaughterhouse at the back, and the slaughterhouse is still there, but it's not used, it's not licensed. And the field at back is where he put beef cattle. He bought them at Bakewell Market, fatstock, and slaughtered them at night to supply Winster with meat. And then there's the Bowling Green. Robert Oliver was there when I was a lad. Several people have took it over, you know, the Bowling Green, different people, and Robert Oliver, he was there years and years. And then Dick Fearn took it over. Mrs Marsland used to live in Winster Hall, and when she died Tom Edward Gregory bought it, on the Main Street, for £2,000, and sold it to Friden brickworks for £10,000, because they wanted to put the prisoners-of-war [displaced persons and refugees] in there, this last war - Poles, Danes, Germans and all sorts. One married Betty Burton down the road, from the shop. And Billy Foxlow, he had three beautiful daughters, and two of them married two Germans, and they went to America. All the men used to work at Friden in the brick factories and what not, and somewhere to roost at night and drink. [John Millward]

John Wild.

John Wild was a miner at Mill Close. He used to be in the engine room, like an engineer. He worked for the engineer. I can remember him going off to work and coming in. He was also King of the Morris Dancers for many years. [Marion Drinkall]

Eva Webster.

I married a local lass, Eva Webster, from Elton. She wasn't a farmer's daughter. She were just ordinary – and, actually, not a lot o' interest in cattle. Well, she were from a distance. She didna go near 'em. Oh, she were all right. I miss her, you know. [Tom Wigley]

George Walker, pork butcher.

My father, George Walker, was born in Winster. He went apprentice to a butcher at Matlock Bath. Then he was called up in the War. He served in France. He was a sergeant major. I think he was a sergeant major all his life, 'cause he treated me very strict! He came back safely from the war, and he went into breeding his own pigs up where the ladies toilets are, round the back of the Bowling Green. He had a little croft and he had his own pigs. Cured all his own bacon down in the cellar. I can see him now, as a child. The water used to run into the cellar, and he'd be standing on blocks of wood rubbing the salt for hour after hour into the bacon, because it was cured in them days. It wasn't like it is today, just dipped in brine. It was really cured. It was cool in the cellar, but he left it for weeks, this bacon with the salt on. It was beautiful, really good. The hams, they'd all hang

> *Winster Wisdom: 'Always keep a little money*
> *that doesn't see daylight.'*

up round the cellar. There were no fridges. Then he'd have his sausage machine and a big old copper. He had to light a fire and my mother would have all the ingredients for brawn - all the pig's head, the feet, the parts that you couldn't cut up for a joint, you'd make the brawn. My dad would be grinding the sausage machine - I could hear that when I was in bed - and making the sausages. He even made his own skins out of the intestines for the sausages, not like they are today. All that would be going on - savoury ducks, everything. I spent very little time helping. I used to clear off, because I hadn't room anywhere to put a book. And I used to go up to my mum's aunt, who lived in the village, where we used to play at cards. I used to go home about half-past-eight for bed and take the dog up with me. It was a poor life for me. My parents had never no time. They were good parents. My dad was strict, my mother wasn't. But it was hard times. As a pork butcher he had little competition. Stephen Rains sold beef and lamb, Stanley Boam beef. Stanley Boam's shop was where Moot House now is. And then there was Blackwell's. Then there was George Will. He had a little shop. He did sell all sorts of things, George did, mainly beef. And Blackwell's was in the Main Street, opposite where Gwen McManus now lives. He moved there from a premises on East Bank. Stephen Rains' shop is now the garage of Roselea Cottage, but, after Rains vacated it, my father took it over as a slaughterhouse. There were no rules and regulations in them days, like you've got to have sinks here and water there. No, he just got on with the job. He killed his pigs. And I'll tell you, this particular time he was fetching it from up the Headlands with a rope round its nose, and, of course, it was squealing its head off. This old lady came down the street on a bicycle, and she said to my dad, 'I'm going to report you to the police.' So my dad said, 'Get on with it.' Of course, she went to Mr Hannigan, the local bobby, and he came laughing. He said, 'Oh dear, I've had this old lady, George. I'll 'ave to do something about it. She's reported you for the pig squealing.' He said, 'We've got to draw a pig and the rope and how you've tied it up.' So my dad said, 'Well, we'll 'ave a go.' I can see it now. They were laughing all the time about this pig, and, of course, nothing came of it, because any pig squeals when you're trying to pull it. So he heard nothing more of it. It's funny though. My dad, although he was a pork butcher and he killed his pigs, he couldn't kill a lamb or a dog. People thought, because he'd got a humane killer, he could just put them to sleep. But no way could he kill a dog or a lamb. [Dot Fearn]

Miss Winfield.

When I lived at the Croft End we used to go and spend pennies at Miss Winfield's or Mrs Allen's. One day Jessie had got a penny to get some sweets. I hadn't any money, but we went in Miss Winfield's and she showed us every sweet she'd got in the shop. Then I turned round to Jessie and I said, 'We'll go to Mrs Allen's!' And she told my mother, I can remember that. I was four. My mother ran at us with a brush. She said it was washday and Miss Winfield was busy. You got quite a lot for a penny. They used to wrap paper round their fingers and make a bag. [Mildred Witham]

The village policeman.

The first one I remember was Bobby Wells. He did Winster, Birchover and Elton. When I was a boy in Birchover it was Bobby Wells who kicked your backside and battered you round the earhole, no messing. Then it was Mr Hannigan. After he went it got a bit more modern. They always patrolled with the bike. The Police Station was operational from Bakewell. When they built the council houses there was the Police House, a cell where you could lock somebody up in it. They used to have something there where they could apprehend. The Police House was always the second council house past Leacroft Garage. [Roy Walters]

'then the police got
a bit more modern'

John Rowland.

John Rowland was a saddler in Winster. He sold shoes and that, yes. He was a lovely gentleman. He was very good to the children. He used to buy them an ice cream when Mazza came round with his ice cream cart. We used to congregate round and he'd buy us an ice cream. He used to go visiting people, and he'd come to Vernon House and used to just stand - I can see him now - with his arm on the sideboard talking. He'd stand for an hour or two probably - it seemed a long time as a child - and off he'd go. When he was older he was ill and couldn't look after himself, and my mother looked after him until he died. He was buried in Winster. His grave is at the bottom right near the door of Dr Stoker's house. [Marion Drinkall]

Mates.

Bill Mosley lived down Pump Lane. It was a little house and he worked at Mill Close Mine. He were in the war. He volunteered himself, although he were getting on a bit. He used to get a lot of beer, and I think him and the wife had a bit of an argument and he went and enlisted. He survived the war. I've got a photo of him in my book at Mill Close Mine, where he's ready for going down the mine with lamp. Jimmy Wood and this man, Bill Mosley, I'm telling you about, were ever such big friends. They were always together at weekends – ever such big beer drinkers together - and both worked down mine. And they were both on same shift. You never saw one without the other. He were a grand chap and he used to think the world of me and my mate, George Waller. And he always said, 'When anything happens to me, you and George Waller, I want you to carry me.' And we did. [Bert Boam]

Ben Clay and his coffin.

Ben used to stand on the market. He was always looking for a bargain, was Ben. I don't know how it came about, but I think it was somebody from Stanton had got a coffin for sale, and Ben bought it. He had a bargain. It was in the front for about twenty years waiting for him to die. Coffins used to be wheeled to church on a bier, a trolley with wheels. They had bearers at the side pushing it down the Main Street. [Dot Fearn]

Landlord of the Crown.

There used to be a big water trough outside the Crown, a big stone one, and on top there was another tank, which fetched all the water off the roof. In 1945 Mr Stone was the landlord. His grandson was very young, and he dropped his pocket-knife in one of these tanks of water. Of course, his granddad went in - a very cold day - to fetch it out, up to his shoulders in cold water,

'a bargain from Stanton'

and he fell ill after that and it turned to cancer. Then, of course, he died at the Crown, and that's while I was in the army. His son, George Will Stone, he was in the army too. They sent a telegram following round where he were in Germany trying to pick him up, saying his father was ill and could he come home at once. By the time he'd landed home he went in the doorway and said, 'Where's my Dad?' And they told him he'd just been buried. Of course, George Will broke down. Mr Stone died in 1945 and Mrs Stone carried it on until 1947. She'd had enough by then. [Bill Slaney]

Stephen Rains and the horse that knew its way home.

Stephen Rains used to collect spare meat from the other two butchers, and he used to take it with the horse and trap to Chesterfield and sell it. And then it come twelve o'clock, all the meat as he'd got left he used to put it up for auction, and you'd bid for it. So they didn't have to have any left. There were never any meat left after Saturday. And after he'd sold all his meat, he'd go to the Crown and Cushion – I think it were – and stop there and keep drinking and drinking till about six o'clock at night, sometimes later. Then he used to come home with horse and trap. And horse knew his road that well, with going continuously, he used to bring himself home. Stephen Rains didn't drive him. He was slumped on the seat and the reins were lying slack, but the horse knew his own way. And he used to land back in Winster at Cauldwell's, right at door. And someone used to help him out of trap and back home. [Bert Boam]

The shy little organist.

We used to go twice every Sunday to Sunday School, and, this particular Sunday, Miss Buxton, the old lady that was in charge - she was the old post lady - she said, 'Hey, Mrs Boam the organist, she can't come t'day. She's not well. Is any of you girls here will come and play for us this afternoon?' There was dead silence. In a little while I said, 'Well, Miss Buxton, I've only just learned to play four hymn tunes. If the preacher can find some words to go to that I'll have a try.'

She said, 'Alright, m'wench, get'th stool'. So I did. It was a Mr George Scriven from Youlgreave who was the preacher, and I remember what he'd chose. I came down and I felt quite proud of m'self. Anyway, sitting round the table at home, teatime, my brother Harry said,

'the shy little organist'

'Hey mum, what d'think? Our Bessie played th'organ this afternoon. She did make a mess of it!' I started to cry. I wouldn't go back.

I can see my father parading round the room now. He said, 'This is a bit of a rum 'un, this is a bit of a rum 'un'. Well, our Harry said, 'We'st 'ave to go without her'. So my mum stopped with me. Anyway, nothing was said when they got back at night. We always used to have family prayers, and then Harry said, 'Mum, what d'yer think? The preacher prayed for 'the shy little organist' tonight.' Well, dead silence. Not another word was said, and off I got to bed. All that week it troubled me. Mr Scriven prayed for the shy little organist, and I let them down. Anyway, I goes off to Sunday School as usual the next Sunday morning and afternoon. In the afternoon service Miss Buxton says 'Well, m'lass, you'll 'ave t'get on organ again. Mrs Boam's not back.' So, of course, I did, and that's where I gradually got my confidence. I was shy and timid before then. But that's when I really felt that the Lord was calling me to do that little job. And it was shortly after that that my mother died. That background helped us all through. [Bessie Thorpe]

Attendance at church.

There used to be a lot of people in church on Sunday - pews and pews full, a very big attendance. My mother used to say when Smiths were at Westhills they filled one pew. Every Sunday they came from the farm and filled one pew. When the Manor, the old people's home, was owned by the Thompsons - when my mother was a child, this was - she had maids for everything, and she insisted they all went. My mother used to tell us. She insisted they all went to church on a Sunday morning, and they filled a pew, all the staff did. They had bonnets on and all dressed up. A lot of private houses had maids. My mother worked at the Archway. A lot of them had maids. [Mildred Witham]

Locked in the church.

We used to have to go to church every Sunday. We were in the choir, and after choir at church, at night, we used to keep pushing one another in those yew trees, head first. We locked the caretaker in one night and nobody dare go and let her out. We locked her in church. There were no lights, you know, only candles. Anyway, I plucked up courage to go home and tell my dad. He did carry on, my dad did. [Hedley Boam]

Sunday School.

I came to Sunday School from Westhills, and I used to take some friends home for tea. My mother believed in Sunday School, but my mother and father didn't go to church a lot, only on special occasions. They were always too busy. We were farming up there, you see, and then he left that and worked at Mill Close Mine, and mum used to help on the farm. Sunday School was in the afternoon. The vicar we had at that time was very strict, and we had exams and everything, and you got medals if you passed these exams that he gave you. [Mildred Witham]

A Methodist Sunday.

Mum Gregory was a Sunday School teacher. She tells me she was first taken to Sunday School when she was three. She started to teach when she was sixteen, and I think she was seventy-six when she stopped taking Sunday School classes. Both mum and dad Gregory were in the choir. Sunday School at half-past-ten in the morning was just for the children, with Mr Hodgkinson. In the afternoon we used to come across here to West Bank at half-past-one and have a service. Mum took the infants, Miss Heathcote took the older ones, Auntie Lilian took the older girls, and Mr Hodgkinson took the older boys. When Joan Hodgkinson was there she did take a class, but she had to go away on war work. I remember mum in the little room, Joan on the stage, Miss Heathcote in the other little room, Auntie Lilian at the front of the main hall and Mr Hodgkinson at the back taking afternoon Sunday School. It couldn't have lasted an hour, because we had to go up the paths and be at the chapel for the afternoon service at half-past-two. If we didn't have the preacher for tea, we always went for a walk round the New Road. If it wasn't too nice a day, we'd cut through Oddo, but if

Mazza's motorbike ice cream cart, c. 1940. Eric Brassington (left),
Geoffrey Barnsley, Mazza, Linda Ellis, Mrs Mary Ellis and Ken Marshall.

it was a nice day you'd go all the way round the New Road, down the street,
and back home for tea. If the preacher was billeted for tea, you didn't get your
walk. You entertained the preacher, gave them their tea, and back up to the
service - six o'clock in the winter and half-past-six in the summer. If it was the
minister, you had the extra best china. [Muriel Gould]

Sunday School Anniversary.

Easter Sundays at the chapel were always special occasions, because it was Prize
Giving. Then there was Sunday School Anniversary. It's just about gone now,
but everybody used to come from far and wide – all the relations and friends. I
came from Birchover to Winster Anniversary with my mother for as long as I
can remember. When I got married I still carried on. We always came for our tea
at Mrs Gregory's, my Auntie Nancy's, and then we used to walk back. Birchover's
was May, and Winster Chapel always shut for Birchover's Sunday School Anniversary, where Birchover shut for Winster Anniversary. They all had them –
Winster, Birchover, Elton. The Reform Chapel did as well, and we used to shut
in the afternoon for the Reform Chapel, and they did the same back for us. It

was a big thing. Everybody had new clothes on that day. You went along and you got your first pair of long trousers on Anniversary Day. [Roy Walters]

The Sunday School treat.

We had tea in the chapel, and then we went up to the Treat Field and played all these games. The Treat Field was up past the Rock Field, and as we were coming away Mr Rains - he was a farmer, and I think he lived on the moors somewhere - he came with a churn of milk. He gave you a mug, or two mugs, of milk, if you wanted. We played different games with bat and ball. As the team were running round you had to keep hitting the ball and be quick - very much like rounders. Then, if you wanted to go and try to play cricket, you could try your hand at that. Afterwards we came away with a bag that was filled with nuts, biscuits, sweets and all sorts. Tired out we were. [Dolly Brassington]

Carol Singing.

The Methodist Chapel used to go round the village every Christmas Day – start at nine o'clock and go right round the village singing carols and finish up on the Flat at four o'clock. Some started at nine o'clock and went straight through, but we used to slip off for an hour, because my mother used to get Christmas lunch ready for us, and after that we'd go back again. [Anne Walters]

The vicar and the piano.

Mr Britton, the vicar, wasn't one of my favourite people, and, the best of it is, our family were regular customers - if you could call us that. My dad was in the choir for 47 years and me and my mum we used to go, and we went to Sunday School. Confirmation, too. Well, my dad was on the Burton Institute Trust, and there was a piano given in memory of some soldier, who was called Heathcote. On the front of the piano was a plaque incorporating his memory. Each time anybody hired the hall they paid 5s to the vicar, and that 5s was meant to go towards tuning and looking after the piano.

Anyway, one day the piano had gone. Nobody knew where. So my dad went to the vicar. He wouldn't say. It was in the newspapers. We had the Daily Express, the Daily Mail and the Derbyshire Times saying 'Where has it gone?' My dad said it was the principle of the thing, and 'If it's the last thing I do, I shall find out about this piano.' Anyway, my dad got the deacon, or somebody who was higher up than the vicar, and he came. Of course, he got to the bottom of it.

They found out that Mr Britton, the vicar, had sold the piano to a pub at Matlock Bath. I've forgotten how much. It was very little, but he'd kept the money. Anyway, they did get the money back and, of course, the plaque. But he wasn't very pleased about it, my dad. But my dad was straight John Bull. There was no messing with him, and he was as honest as the day. [Dot Fearn]

> *Winster Wisdom: 'Better belly bust than good stuff wasted.'*

A wedding-day incident.

My dad had another run-in with the vicar on my wedding day. The church was full. I had 102 guests - that was without the village people, who always went to look at a wedding. Well, I think the vicar thought, 'Now I've got my church full' - this was Mr Britton again – 'I'll cash in on them.' So me and my husband sat in the choir stalls and he sent the collection plate round. He'd have quite a lot of money. Anyway, my dad didn't like to cause a commotion with it being the wedding day, but he said, 'Wait till I get him in my shop.' I think if he'd have had his humane killer there, he'd have shot him. And he told him it wasn't fitting to do that, to send a plate round, and it was very, very bad. Anyway, he got away with it - for a few pound of sausages and what-have-you. He was a vicar alright! [Dot Fearn]

Santa at the Bowling Green.

A good many years ago - I think I was about four years of age [1917] - I was at the Bowling Green with my father. He was playing a cornet in the band. I can remember I was sat outside, because I wasn't old enough to go inside, and Santa Claus came down the steps from what was then the club room. He had a big sack on his back. He'd been delivering toys for the children and he came out to me. My father had given me a money box, like a little postbox, and Santa Claus took it round the pub and brought it out, and it was full of pennies. [Bill Slaney]

An early road accident.

I'll never forget. My grandmother had the chip shop across the road from Post Office, where I lived. There was a horse and carriage. They used to call it a 'tub'. It was like a round affair with wheels on. I was no more than five [1914], and I came running down to cross the road to my granny's. Well, this tub and pair was coming down the street and I got knocked down by the horses. I could see under the horse's belly. The carriage went right over me and never killed me. Mary Dale took me to Whitworth, but I had only bruises and cuts. [Bert Boam]

Whips and tops.

I can remember before the road outside here was tarmacked it was just rough cobblestones. There was nowhere to play hopscotch - there was no surface, it was just rough. That was a long time ago, perhaps sixty years, because, I remember, the shop next to Market House Cottage had whips and tops, and as soon as there was a flat surface, then we could have a whip and top. We all finished up with whips and tops. It was lovely! As I said before, you couldn't play football. It was dreadful! It was sandy, and when the wind blew there was all this dust. Then, of course, Mr Thorpe, the Special Constable, had the first bus in the village. It was nice to have a nice smooth ride, instead of a bumpy one over these rocks and stones. [Dot Fearn]

Sledging, skipping and dolls.

The youths used to stand outside the Post Office. We used to play outside - hopscotch, whip-and-top, sledging in the winter down the Horsecrofts. We used to sledge down East Bank in the dark. I distinctly remember one time when we'd got candles in jam jars so we didn't go into the side. That was lovely. We weren't very popular for it, but we did it. We used to play 'tally-ho!' That was in two groups of people, and one tried to find the other group, going all round the village. People who were trying to find them would say, 'Shout, else we shan't follow', and the other group would have to shout, 'Tally-ho!' We mostly played skipping in the street. A game called 'high-and-low' sometimes would be across East Bank. We'd have long clothes lines, you see, and we'd do the high and low jumping and skipping, and double skipping, and all that.

In the summertime we went up Wyntor Rocks. We used to spend days up there. It was really lovely climbing the rocks. There was one rock that we called a rocking horse, and another one was the rocking chair. You took your dolls up there, or just played hide-and-seek in the rocks. A lot of children played up there. We used to go all over - as far as Lunter Rocks and down to Cratcliffe Rocks and Robin Hood's Stride. Oh yes, and Clough Wood. Lots of parents used to go down there, put a rope round, and drag big logs up, and things like that. As children we used to go and play and probably bring a few sticks back. And I remember the brook. We used to paddle in it, and you could spend ages with a little fishing net, hoping to catch something. But you never saw anything. There was all stones in, and it was lovely to paddle. Further down, as you got nearer where you go to Mill Close Mine, there was this massive big iron pipe that we used to play going through. That was the highlight of the day. [Marion Drinkall]

The Rock Field.

We'd play hide and seek, running up towards the chapel, down the little gennel towards the Flat, round and about there. We had happy times on the Flat. In the summer, from school, we would take our dolls, prams, tea-sets and all our toys up into the Rock Field on the rocks. They would stay up there all night. We seemed to have hot summers then. I don't know if it's imagination or not, but our toys seemed to stay up there a long time. Barbara Foxlow, Maureen Gladwin - we'd spend a lot of time up there. Mum would come to the bottom of the Rock Field and shout when it was lunchtime. We'd go down for lunch and reappear back up there again after lunch. [Eileen Crowder]

Snow.

I've spent hours and hours and hours on the Rock Field, climbing the trees, playing in the caves there. We sledged on the Rock Field, and we sledged on the field at the top of Woolley's Yard, too, and I went over the wall there, cracked my head! In the winter the men couldn't get to work, so they all worked for the Council and cleared the snow, and they were paid by the Council instead of being paid by their own works. There was the big horse-drawn snowplough. [Muriel Gould]

'Kick-can-round-the-Market-House.'

We used to play a game called kick-can. We called it 'kick-can-round-the-Market-House'. We had a can in front of the Market House, just any old tin can, and we had to peep round the sides, and, if you saw someone, you just had to shout their name and say, 'One, two, three...' and then they had to be 'on'. Then we played hare-and-hounds, often boys against the girls, all over the village, and we would shout, 'Shout else we shan't follow,' and they'd shout, 'Tally-ho!' Of course, by the time we got where they were shouting they'd be some-where else altogether, so really it was just a game that we all wanted to play. We played hopscotch in the street, because there wasn't the traffic in those days, and those who had a car, petrol was rationed, and so they had very little petrol. [Amy Slater]

'kick-can-round-the-Market-House'

'Tally-ho!'

We played kick-can, mithering round Mosley's shop. We played mostly round the Market House. There was the one where you stood with your hands to your back and somebody hit you, and you had to guess who it was. And there was a game called kick-knock. You used to all run behind the Market House and peep, and if they saw you, they called your name out, and you had to go and stand at the front. And somebody had to try and rescue you by banging on the Market House door. For kick-can we kicked this can up and down the village. We also played 'tally-ho!' all round the village. In this game you were set into two gangs. One set off and the other had to come and find you. You used to have to shout, 'Shout else I shan't follow.' The ones that were hiding had to shout, 'Tally-ho!' But then you'd run before they found you. We weren't supposed to go out too far, but we'd sometimes end up on top of the Bank, but we weren't supposed to do that when it got dark. [Muriel Gould]

Games and maypole dancing.

We used to play hopscotch, whip-and-top up the Street and maypole dancing. Mrs Fletcher, the doctor's wife, was a wonderful lady. She learnt us maypole dancing. And we used to have a Fun Day at the Vicarage, and we'd do maypole dancing and all sorts of country dancing. There were side-shows and all things like that. But they didn't stretch it out like they do now. It was one big day and it was held on the playing fields, the recreation ground, where the council houses are now. [Dot Fearn]

Playing on the tip.

The tip on Bonsall Lane was a breeding ground for rats, and we used to go with air guns, shooting at these rats on a Sunday. On the tip itself there were railway lines - somebody had put them in - and an old truck on the lines. One Sunday Nanny Boam had bought me a brand new white shirt. She said, 'You're not to go near that tip.' Anyway, we went up, and Alex Fairey was with us. He were the boggie, and he shot the railway truck along the track. If you got hit with it, it would have killed you. Lo and behold, it came at me and took hold of my brand new shirt. I daren't go home. It had marked it, you see. I'd be about twelve, I should think [1927].

On one occasion the tip was on fire. That was how they used to get rid of the rubbish. It was burning underneath, you know, so far down. I thought there was no fire, you see, so we pushed a wheelbarrow, and I went to tip it up. But instead of that my foot went in, into burning ashes. I wasn't very old, fourteen probably. We couldn't get my shoe off, and there's still a scar left on my foot. We had the doctor, but you had to pay for them. Betty Greatorex's mother [Georgina Greatorex], she got hold of me when I came down the Bank, and she said, 'You'll have to put something round that as soon as ever you can.' When you get burnt it forms a bubble. Betty made me put this bag on to make it airtight. Then I had to walk all the way home. [Hedley Boam]

Walking to school on market days.

Winster was a very old market village, and when it was market day we used to come down over the Croft and down East Bank, because the Street was so full of animals – cows and sheep. More of the sheep were down East Bank. We were afraid of the animals – that's why we went down the Croft. [Dolly Brassington]

First day at school.

When I was old enough to go to school, the first day I went I had a friend to take me. And coming back from school he took me to the abattoir where they were killing a cow, and he helped to pull on the rope. I was a little bit frightened so I ran home. That was the first day at school. [Bill Slaney]

Pupils from outlying farms.

School was a lot different, because, being on a moor farm, children think you have no one behind you, and so they think they can bully you and get away with it - which some of them did, actually. But Winster was quite different. They seemed to be more one-together, the children. There was one boy that tried to bully a little bit the first day, but, of course, all the others would stick up for you, because you were new. One of the things I can remember was having to walk from Gratton Moor to Middleton School and Elton School. At first I went to Middleton, and then father thought it was nearer to Elton. But it wasn't! I used to take long strides to get there quicker. Then I realised the others were taking three strides to my one, so I had to, sort of, try and walk a little bit more lady-like. [Amy Slater]

The village school after the First World War.

In 1924, when I first started school, the room that's now the kitchen was the cloakroom, 112 pegs for the clothes to be hung up in this room. Everybody, as soon as they started school, were given a certain number peg to put their clothes on. As they got bigger they got changed, and infants took bottom ones and we took high-up ones.

Straight from the main entrance you went into the infants' classroom. We used to be all in rows straight across, facing the window looking up the fields, and there used to be about thirty little forms that had wooden planks at front. In the other room they used to have inkpots as well, but not here. We used to have crayons. At very first we used chalk with slates. We used to play with beads and things like that when we first came, then we moved up a little bit and some more, and then we moved up again, until you'd been here about two or three year, and then you moved through into the other room. There were nothing in here, only just forms.

You could seat thirty, and they used to have room at front. Teacher used to stand there under the window. The blackboard used to go there in that corner. Of course, they used to think it was taking too much room up. Talk about shortage of books, I think there's no shortage today! We used to take everything with us. We used to have to keep 'em y'sen in a tidy heap.

There were three main groups – the infants, juniors, and seniors. Altogether there were more than a hundred being taught by three teachers and Headmaster. All through the school you were moved from class to class, depending on how quickly you learned. There were three classes in the infants, but only one teacher for them all. I remember it was so crowded you couldn't move, and no talking was allowed. In the big room there was the juniors. They were four classes and two teachers. The seniors were in four classes - four groups with one teacher. There was less in the top one - only about five or six – because people used to leave before they got to it, depending on where your birthday fell. You were in here for four years, and you left at fourteen, or before fourteen, if your birthday came just before term. You used to leave four times a year in them days, because there were four terms. We used to go back in August - you only had a month. You got two terms in by Christmas. Then you went to Easter. Then you went to Summer holidays. There were no half-term holidays, only half a day for Shrove Tuesday. As soon as it got wintertime and we got a dark, dull day, if it got very dark we used to get sent home, because you'd no lighting at all in the school - none at all, nothing. But the school was heated by coke.

A lot of what we learned was generally about the British Empire in them days. Empire Day 24th May, Queen Victoria's birthday, and then Oak and Apple Day - that was the 27th May. If anybody hadn't got a piece of oak on them, they got stung by a nettle.

We learned tables in infants. There wouldn't be as many dunces then! Went up to twelve times in the infants. Last thing we did before we came out of the infants, we had to know us tables. There was a small shop at the front with biscuits and pounds of sugar, and that, with prices on them. They used to tell you to fetch a basket and bring something and reckon 'em up. That was sums. There was a little school library, but where it went I don't know. We used to have assembly every morning as soon as we came in. All the lot used to come in here from infants, and all lot used to stand in here just in this room. [Ernest Hope]

Celebrating Shrove Tuesday.

When it was Shrove Tuesday they used to ring a bell at eleven o'clock, and the Headmaster at Winster School had already picked two of the strongest lads out. And we used to go up to Mrs Thompson at the Manor, and she would give us two great big baskets of oranges, one for each pupil. And then, as soon as you'd had your orange and the bell had rung, you used to have the half-day off. You used to have your shuttle cock, spinning tops and marbles. [Bert Boam]

Lessons.

I liked school. You see, I was an only child, and to be with other children, I enjoyed it. We went to cookery every Tuesday down at Two Dales, and that was a nice ride out. Swimming on a Friday at the Whitworth. The cookery lessons were where Hayes Bakery is now, and we had laundry lessons as well. I also had private piano lessons with Miss Beresford, and that used to be over the top of George Will Stone's butcher's shop. It was half-a-crown for half-an-hour, and that was a lot of money. And then I went to Mrs Drinkall at Eagle Tor. That was one-and-six for half-an-hour. [Dot Fearn]

Discipline at school.

Discipline had to be good, else you'd wing through that door to the headmaster. If you talked you used to get fifty lines, and if they caught you talking after that it was doubled every time, if anybody talked in class. You tried to get out of them if you could, but the teacher this side used to see that you did them. But when you went to the headmaster's side you used to forget, and you'd just walk out at playtime and get away with it. Sidney Thorpe was the headmaster all the time I was here. He'd only just come. He used to live at School House, and then he flitted up to Lyndhurst on West Bank. Sometimes we used to have the cane - six strokes on your hands and then turn round and smile at him, and that made him worse. [Ernest Hope]

Memories of teachers.

I was born where Gill lives, Market House at the bottom of East Bank. My dad was a butcher there. I went to Winster School until I was fourteen. Lots of happy memories of that school. The headmaster was Mr Thorpe. There was Miss Howes and Miss Williams, and they used to lodge with Miss Smith, where Nancy and George Staton lived [The Old House, East Bank]. Miss Smith used to put these teachers up Monday to Friday. She gave them bed and breakfast.

Mr Thorpe was very strict, and not always fair with his punishment. If there was two talking he'd have you both out. He used the stick. That used to be kept

Teachers at Winster School, c. 1920.
Headmaster Sidney Thorpe with Miss Smith
(left), Mrs Hooker and Mrs Webster.

down the side of the black-board. It was a thick stick. It didn't half use to hurt! He used it on me once. I was going in from playtime and Teddy Dale jumped on my back and we both fell on the floor. So we both got it. [Dot Fearn]

Two contrasting headteachers.

The headteacher was Mr Sidney Thorpe. I was a bit frightened of him, really, to be honest. Maybe it was just me that was timid, but I was quite frightened of him. He seemed to shout a lot and always looked very stern. I never saw him smile, actually. Our next headmaster was wonderful. One thing I remember about the new headmaster, Mr Bell, was that in Mr Thorpe's day when you said, 'Please Sir, I'm sorry, but I didn't understand,' you were very likely to get the stick. So I never dared say I didn't understand, and I just had to fumble through things. But this time, when Mr Bell was there, I didn't understand something that was on the board about a sum. And he said, 'Now, does everyone understand?' So I very timidly put my hand up, and I can remember to this day there was almost a gasp, because they wondered what was going to happen. He said, 'I'm really pleased that someone said that, because it's no good sitting there and not knowing what you're doing.' So he went straight through the whole thing again. Of course, that broke a lot of barriers down with us, right in the beginning. He was a very nice teacher. He did give the stick, but only when even the children thought it was necessary. He was very fond of singing, and one of the boys thought he was a bit of a favourite and thought he could play about in singing. Mr Bell told him several times, 'Now, that's the last time I'm going to tell you'. Of course, this boy still thought he could play around, and so he said

'Come out' and he gave him the stick. He said when we were doing lessons he expected us to be quiet, and he expected us to get on with the lessons. But he was very, very fair. I think even this boy realised afterwards that he'd done wrong. [Amy Slater]

Discovered smoking in the toilets.

The children used to get up to all kinds of tricks. I remember the boys smoking in the urinal one day. What they didn't realise was that the teachers could see through the window the smoke curling up, and they could see who the boys were. We were in assembly one day and Mr Bell said, 'Come out those boys who have been smoking in the toilets.' I think eventually about three came out. We could see the others grinning, because we knew who they were. So he told them that they could smoke at home with their parents' consent, but they weren't allowed to smoke on school premises. He also said, 'Are there any more?' No-one came out. Then he said, 'Come out so-and-so and so-and-so.' He knew exactly who had been smoking, and when he gave them the stick he only gave possibly one stroke, but the cane nearly swished in two. They knew they'd had it, and they knew they deserved it. The amazing thing was, really, those boys knew they deserved it. So, really, there was very little bitterness towards the teacher. [Amy Slater]

From primary to secondary school.

I went to Winster C of E, a lovely school. The headmaster's name was Sidney Thorpe. He also had a brother that kept one of the grocery shops, called Robert Thorpe. I believe that was taken over by a Mosley. I think there were four classes - quite big classes, well attended. Also, the headmaster used to give the cane. Then I went to Ernest Bailey's at Matlock when I was about twelve, where I had to pay a fee. We wore a uniform there - panamas in the summer and felt in the winter. I left when I was about fifteen. [Phyllis Taylor]

Leaving school.

I went to the school just up the road. There were none of this jumping on a bus and going to big school - none of that then. It was just village school. I left school at fourteen. I were a man when I were fourteen. Old folk used to think you were. You used to work like a donkey. There were no wage. I used to ask my dad for a bit o' money. He'd give me a shilling. It used to cost a shilling on bus down Matlock. When bus firm had shilling that were it. I'll tell you how I used to get my money. I used to get rabbits. I used to set hangs every night, and every Sunday I were ferreting with gun. At that time rabbits were about 9d and 1s each. In a week I could get as many as a fellow could carry up there in a bag. This man used to come from Sheffield. He used to like his rabbits. He were very disappointed when I'd got none. But it were very, very rare as I'd got none. Lads I used to go out wi', I had more blinkin' money than they had, 'cos of the rabbits. Then I set up with fowls on my own and I started with pigs, and I had a little banking account of my own. [Tom Wigley]

Coal deliveries.

Mr Heath at Winster had a man working with him who used to cart coal from Darley Dale Station to Winster and then tip it up in the street. That's how the people in the village got their coal. There isn't many people in Winster who've got a back door. So when the coal came you'd tip the coal in front of the door in the street, near the causeway, and, as soon as they brought a load, either the man or the woman would start getting it in. You could only bring 10 cwt a time, so you'd see a load of coal here and a load of coal there, and most of the way up the street most days someone, somewhere, would have some coal outside. They used to take it through the house and they'd have some kind of a place to just stack the coal. It was mostly in rather big lumps, so people could stack it up like that. [Bert Boam]

Coal under the stairs.

People used to fetch coal from the station with horses and carts. They would just dump it in the street, and you had to get to do yourself, bring it in. It wasn't in sacks, just loose, just great big lumps of shiny coal, massive lumps of beautiful shiny coal, that you don't get to-day. A nice big lump on your fire was better. It lasted longer. If you'd got a garden, that's where you would store it. If not, they used to have it under the stairs, the coalhouse under the stairs. Coal was delivered twice a year probably. You used to get a load and it would last.

We used to have a fire in most rooms. Even upstairs there's a fireplace. Some of the old cottages you'll find a fireplace in every bedroom. We'd go up to bed at night to a fire. We used coal for cooking, heating, everything - oven, boiler and open fire. One side was the oven, the other side was where you had your hot water boiler. You had your kettle on the fire. There was a rail across with a hook where you could put your kettle, and there was always hot water for your tea or anything. There used to be an iron bar with holes, and

'they cleaned them with a holly bush'

you could hook it higher or lower, so it was quite easy really. If you wanted it very hot you made sure that your flues were all cleaned out. They used to clean them with a bush, a holly bush, if you hadn't got any rods and a brush. Cleaning was done by any of us that would do it. We'd fall out over things like that - cleaning, dirty jobs. We used to try to pass them on to each other.

People used to clean their own chimneys - they had to do. And they used to have a lot of chimneys on fire. There was always someone's chimney on fire, and then it didn't need sweeping. Nowadays if you get a chimney on fire there's fire brigades and everything, but then no one used to bother. The atmosphere in the village with all these coal fires was very foggy. All the people who hire the cottages now want a coal fire, so they're just going back to what it was. [Mavis Corker]

Counting the bags.

There were quite a few people came into the village with coal, but my earliest memories are Smiths of Darley Dale. I think they supplied most of the village. We had a coalhouse in the garden. If you ordered four bags, my mother used to watch them go by the window and count them to make sure she'd got four bags, because they'd tip the coal into the coal house in a heap, take the sack back on to the lorry. If you'd got a heap of coal, looking at it you can't really tell if you've got three bags or four, but to make sure, most people used to count. We'd have lump coal mainly. The ashes that were taken out of the grate were sieved into a dustbin and thrown among the coal. If you wanted to have a good fire you put a big lump of coal on and back it up with the ashes. [Dot Fearn]

A coal fire upstairs.

Heating was with coal. A delivery man came round. I don't know who the first man would be, but for years and years it was a man from Ambergate called Byard. We had him for a long, long time until he retired. He delivered big lump coal, huge lumps. The best household lump coal, that's what my mother used to buy. It was delivered into the house. We kept it under the stairs at the start, and then we got a coalhouse out at the back. It was used for heating and cooking. The only time I remember having fires upstairs was when someone was ill. If you were ill in bed you had a coal fire upstairs. When you went to bed at night you were kept warm with blankets and hot water bottles. [Mildred Witham]

Cooking with coal.

We had two fireplaces. We had one in the kitchen and one in the living room. The one in the kitchen was black leaded with a side oven and a boiler, and it had got a hook hanging and a bar that you could put across your fire, so that your kettle or whatever you were using wouldn't be directly on to the coal. If you wanted it to simmer slowly you'd take your hook higher up the chimney. If you wanted to make a rice pudding, then you'd wait until evening when you weren't going to make your fire up, and then put your pudding in the oven. The fire would gradually go out and you'd have a lovely creamy pudding next morning, because it had cooked so slowly. I've never tasted anything like my mum's rice pudding. It was an Excelsior range, black iron edged with steel, which when it was nice and clean it used to shine like silver, a contrast from the black. [Dot Fearn]

Paraffin stoves.

There were also paraffin stoves. They were black, about three or four foot tall, with paraffin and wick. But the smell! You could smell the paraffin all over the house. [Dot Fearn]

Mantles and moths.

There was no electricity, so everyone had to rely, more than anything, on paraffin lamps. They had a mantle, later on as years go by, and they used to be a really good light. Then the gas came along, and then electricity, of course. In Winster they got these gas lamps put on, and Fred Wilson, he were the man that used to go round lighting them and turning them off with a pole, like. He'd go round and turn them off about ten o'clock at night. Then the houses got 'em in. The gas just used to flare up and open out a bit, like. Then others there'd be a mantle on. But these gas mantles, if a moth touched them, or anything like that, it broke right away. A little fly just touched them, they'd collapse. [Bert Boam]

Brighter and better.

When gas came it was definitely better. I remember that you could have a gas cooker, and it was better than fiddling about with your fire. We might put a penny in the meter and then it went to a shilling in the meter. And when gas came the lighting changed. It used to be a naked flame and then we had a mantle and then we had the electric. That was brilliant. Everything was brighter and better. [Mavis Corker]

Singeing the hairs off a pig.

Gas could be regulated easier. You'd only got to turn on the tap. I'm sure there must have been a lot of calamities in the cooking when they had to rely on coal, because plenty of people now can't cook with gas. So, really, getting to know your oven was a big thing. Some people might be intimidated by something new like gas, such as stoves blowing up and all that sort of thing. The lighting that you had in the house changed too. You had mantles. Some people just had a flame, but you didn't get the same light as what you did with a mantle. I know my dad had got one in the back kitchen. It was just a flame that he used for singeing the hairs off a pig, which helped, because you didn't get hairs in your brawn then. Before that we relied on candles or lamps. Some of these cottages are so low that to have a gas lamp you must have had either to duck - because they did come down quite a bit - or knock the mantle off. I don't remember, but I think some people might have had them on the wall, because the ceilings were so low it was safer. At bedtime you'd probably have a candle. To have gas upstairs was a luxury. [Mildred Witham]

The lamplighter.

The lamps were lit by gas, and so there was the young man lived next door, a Mr George Burnett, he used to be the lamplighter. He lived in the police house. He was the policeman's son. He was delicate, and my father used to pay him twelve shillings every Saturday night. I can see him giving him this now. Of course, it was voluntary. They had to go round collecting in the money, so two or three of them went round. It always used to be a joke with my dad. He went to one certain place - I won't say, but I know who it was. He said, 'I'm round on behalf of, collecting for the street lights.' 'Oh,' he said, 'I canna find yer anythin'. But it's so lovely. Lamp's just outside my window. I've no need t'light me light to get undressed to go to bed.' [Bessie Thorpe]

Lantern slides and moving pictures.

And then electricity came along about the time of the First World War. Same as at churches and such as that, they used to have these magic lanterns with slides. I don't think, somehow, as it was done by electricity. I'm trying to think how they used to do it when the cinema first started up in Matlock. I think it used to be thre'pence in old money. I can remember a man who projected them on to the screen. He was in this 'ere room doing, so I should think electric must just have been started then. [Bert Boam]

Trouble with the generator.

I had a generator at first, down here [Painter's Way Farm]. It was a Lister Startermatic - until it went wrong! We used to have television with it. When television had finished I used to have to walk straight across house and switch it off. I got Marsdens at Wirksworth to try and put it right, but, oh no, he'd got his book and he were all afternoon looking at this blinkin' book, but he had to go, he couldn't do it. I got brother-in-law, he were a bit electrical. One day, he were determined to do it - to make it start with switch – and, of course, one day he got pliers in his hand and he fixed it into bulb holder. Engine started. He said, 'I've got it! I've got it!' He was jumping about. Now the funny thing about it, as soon as you put bulb in, it were dead. So, I said to him after, 'Do you think it'd be earth?' Then, of course, electric folk come, and they fixed this line down valley. It went to Wensley, and one o' chaps said, 'When we've got connected up, you'll have a better picture on television.' And it were not better picture at all! At one time it used to be lanterns and candles down here - oh yes, I remember that day! You know, old lantern, turn wick up and strike a match, and wind blew it out! [Tom Wigley]

> Winster Wisdom: 'Don't marry for money,
> but love where there is a bit.'

Electrical wiring.

The electricity came to the village before 1930. It was Notts and Derby Electric Company. My father was always a clever man. He used to study electricity, although he hadn't got it himself. He showed me how to wire this house up. That was the first job I ever did. I wired that house under his supervision. I used to go wiring houses and farms and all that. I've done several houses in the village. Then Notts and Derby came and examined all the wiring and checked it, passed it. They said, 'Well Mr Hodgkinson, you'll never need us again. You've made a marvellous job of it.' I wired my Uncle Sam's shop at the top of the street. [Vin Hodgkinson]

Wirelesses.

In the days before they had electricity wirelesses were run on accumulators, and you had to go and charge those. Walter Thorpe used to charge batteries up, and Hodgkinson's in the Street did, too. It was a nuisance, that was, because they were heavy. I think they charged a penny. [Dot Fearn]

To save a penny.

It was a big jump from gas to electricity. You weren't running about with your batteries up to Mr Thorpe to be charged. You'd have an electric radio, electric iron, electric cooker, and immediate light without having to strike matches. It was wonderful! It cost more, so a lot of people would stick to their original grates with the coal, because it would heat your water, heat your room, cook your food all for the same price. At first there were meters, and you'd need just a penny, and if you wanted it to last you'd put in sixpence or a shilling. I think a shilling was the most you could put in. My Auntie lived in Anson Row and her husband worked at Mill Close. She'd sit in the dark until he came home at ten o'clock, and then she'd put a penny in the meter for him to eat his supper - all to save a penny! [Mildred Witham]

A well in the cellar.

My grandmother lived across the road from the Post Office in Winster, where the chestnut tree is and where my brother Randolph lived. In those days there was a passageway where you came in from the footpath, and you went down a passage in the house which led to the back door. Facing you, if you undid that door, there were some steps that led down, and when you went down these steps there was a big well in the bottom. [Bert Boam]

The village pump.

Pump Lane is called Woodhouse Lane now. There used to be a pump at the bottom. It was walled off, like a triangle, and the pump in the centre. It were a big hand-pump, you know, this old-fashioned great big cast iron, it were like that. It was past the last house, where it starts to go down steep. There's a gate across now. This was fenced off just for this pump - just an opening for everybody to walk to go to pump. [Bert Boam]

Hard and soft water.

No one had got water in the house, and you had to go to the stand taps in the village. And if water were frozen up, someone in the village had to make a fire underneath to thaw the water out before you could get any. In summertime - the summers seemed to be that hot and there wasn't the water in these villages - in several villages - Winster was one - you used to run short of water. And I've had to queue up for it, or you had to travel about nearly two miles and go either to Shothouse or go to Eagle Tor at Birchover to fetch it. Their water were soft water, but Shothouse water were hard water. Your mother couldn't wash very well with Shothouse water, because it was hard. And so you used to get Birchover water, which came off of sandstone, which was softer water, and that was better for washing. Yes. It used to come out of the reservoir down the West Bank there, where it's all filled in, sort of thing, now. [Bert Boam]

The tap yard.

You know Woodhouse Lane and it used to be called Pump Lane? I remember the big pump being there. We used to fetch water from a tap. Before we got water in the houses you had to carry water in, but there were stand taps all round the village. There was one on Woolley's Yard - you know, where the garage is, the end house of Andy's there. I told him one day, 'You've disturbed all the tap yard.' I said there was a stand tap there, and that was the tap yard. There was a tap outside the church. It comes down Oddo field, that water. When Roy and Keith built those houses on there, they went on to that water. They're on the other main now down there, but originally they brought water across Roy's field. [Mildred Witham]

'you would have to fetch it from the tap'

The same enamel mug.

We used to have to fetch it, apart from what was in the large tanks. There was one for the bathroom outside, coming off the roof, and the one for the kitchen - a very large one - which stood on the big stone trough just to the side of the kitchen window. All the drinking water had to be carried. If there wasn't enough in the tank for the washing up and things, you would have to fetch it from the tap in the village. The nearest one was next to Stanley House on the side of the wall at the Manor. We used to have to go there. Of course, when it was hot weather there would be only so much allowed, and you would have to queue up to get the water. In the hot weather usually the head boys at school would fetch a couple of buckets of water from the tap that I already mentioned near Stanley House. There used to be two enamel buckets, two enamel mugs, and they used to give us a drink all out of the same mug. We didn't have milk. The only thing we had was Horlicks tablets. We could buy Horlicks tablets. [Marion Drinkall]

Bamboozled and ill-used.

First of all was the water business. In the summertime there used to be an awful shortage of water, and poor Mr Hodgkinson, the Town Clerk, had to come and turn the taps off at nine o'clock in the morning and he wouldn't put them on again until perhaps four. And everybody was allocated one bucket of water at the different taps. So poor Mr Hodgkinson didn't half get bamboozled, ill-used, you know. Anyway, we were the bakery. It was rather difficult for us. My father used to borrow so many - I think, six - milk churns - I can't remember which farmer it was - and they used to have to go down to Grimsby Well and we used to pay 6d a churn for this water. [Bessie Thorpe]

Borrowing churns.

I told you about fetching water from Shothouse Spout, didn't I? When the village got short of water – which was very often – you had to borrow three or four milk churns and shove them in the motor. They were anybody's churns, see. They had dropping points, these farmers did. They put the empty ones out and picked the new ones up. They were for Nestlé's at Ashbourne. You had to be cheeky and go and collar anybody's, so long as you took them back. [Hedley Boam]

When the taps froze.

The taps froze up and we couldn't get water, so the farmers went down to Shothouse Spout with milk churns and their horses and carts and carted water. Well, they'd stand anywhere and sell it 1d a bucket, this water, and, by Jove, weren't they glad of it! It makes you careful when you've no water. [Dot Fearn]

A pipe in the night.

We had a huge water tank just out here, and we relied on rainwater. When nobody was looking my husband would take a pipe from the standpipe on the road over there and fill our big tank - about four or five o'clock in the morning when nobody was looking! Mind, he would have got away with it - he would have got away with murder! They wouldn't have dared say anything. That's how we managed with water. I don't remember when it was laid on. Certainly when we got married, that's how we managed. I think most people would have a little tank. [Marjorie Stoker]

When the taps froze, 1963. George Goodwin (left), Eve Nutt,
Wallace Boam, Agnes and Mary Shepherd, Margery Pickles,
Eunice Vincent, Dorothy Walker, Florence Heathcote,
Ethel Boam, with children Kevin Nutt and David Pickles.

Ben White and his motorbike.

Ben White, the blacksmith, had a motorbike. He was the keeper of the water,
and, if it hadn't have been for him, Winster wouldn't have had any water.
He had to go down every day to Shothouse - where the pumping station is
now – and he had to put so much water into the reservoir that was down West
Bank. He had to pump it up. So that was one reason he had his motorbike,
for there and back, because he never knew when anybody was bringing any
horses or any farm machinery to be mended, 'cause he was very clever that way.
[Gladys Hardy]

An incident at the reservoir.

About 1953 or 1954 - because William was about two or three and Andrew was
about six or seven – Eric, my husband, was working in one of the fields near to
an open reservoir, which was at the top – on Shothouse there – in one of the
fields on the right-hand side. Have you noticed that there's a stile through the

fields, opposite the bottom of Bonsall Lane, and the path goes across the fields? Well, when you've gone across three fields the reservoir is there. Mr White was in charge of all this. He turned the water on. He worked for the Water Board, and he lived in the village. Well, Eric was working in the field and William was with him, but Andrew and another boy, who lived just down here, they were playing around this reservoir and they were throwing grass in and bits of things, throwing stones in, but they'd also found an oil can, and they threw that in. They weren't there long, because as soon as Eric noticed they were there he said, 'Come on off there', thinking they'd fall in. Later that day a very irate Mr White came down to see me saying, 'Your kids have been all over here and they've done this and that, and it's all lying on top o' water, so it'll have to be drained'. So I said, 'Well, you have to do what you have to do. I don't know anything about it.' So I tackled them and said, 'What were you doing up there?' And they said, 'Well, there were some frogs in the water and we were throwing at them.' It was reported in the paper, and there was a great big piece about vandalism on the water. So, of course, I wrote a letter and I said that no vandalism was intended at all. There were frogs in the water. So can you imagine all the fuss. The whole thing was drained. Everybody was boiling the water. Anyway, one of the Parish Councillors at that time - it was the late Eric Shimwell - came up to me and said, 'Don't worry about it, Margaret. The rubbish that came out of that reservoir - old bicycles and you name it - it was all in the bottom.' He said it was a good job they did it! [Margaret Tomlinson]

An ultimatum.

It was 1946, and I had two children by that time, and I had to fetch the water in buckets from up the Bank, where the trough is. Up West Bank there's a trough in the big wall. Well, there was a stand-tap there, and I had to fetch the water from there in buckets. On wash days Eric used to bring me down a churn full of water. He used to roll it down, a churn full, to wash. I used to take my nappies to the stand-tap and rinse them all under the tap. I had an old mangle, because I had no electricity. Then in 1946 I went home to my mother and I left an ultimatum: 'If you don't put the water on, I'm not coming back.' I didn't mean it, of course, but fortunately Eric's older brother, Reg, worked for the Water Board - East Derwent Valley Water Board in those days. I must have motivated them, because they dug a trench across the back of the garden and connected it to the water. It was about 1946. I can't be sure, because I never kept a diary. So I had running water. How marvellous it was! Previously to that I had a big metal tank outside the house, which the roof drained into, and nothing else but a brass tap over an old-fashioned sink. Well, that was alright for the rough work, but it wasn't fit, and it had got tiny red worms, which I later discovered was the larvae of the – what do they call those flies that breed in water? - mosquito larvae. We get immune to them, don't we? So it was a big thing to have water laid on. [Margaret Tomlinson]

A copper in the corner.

To heat the water we had a copper in the corner of the kitchen, with a little fire. A lot of people, same as the Angel there, used to have washhouses - a building outside with these fire copper things in. On bath night you had the tin bath in front of the fire. We used to have a bath about once a week and that was all. We didn't waste water at all. [Mavis Corker]

Washing and bathing.

We'd got a room where my mother washed - the washhouse. We had the copper there, the mangle, the dolly tub, the dolly pegs, the poncher - everything you needed for washing - and the bath hung on the wall. When you were very small you had a smaller bath on the hearth. When you wanted the long one, when you got older, you used it in there out of the copper and that warmed the place up. [Mildred Witham]

Possers and dolly pegs.

Washing was hard work, because all the water had to be carried in to be heated. There were no washing machines, only dolly tubs and dolly pegs. We had a copper in the kitchen at the back, and that had to be filled first. We were living in West Bank then, at the Croft, and the tap was just below the Burton Institute, so it wasn't too far away.

A copper would hold about six buckets of water. It would take some time to heat that up before washing. It was almost a whole day's job. All the clothes were in the dolly tub. We used to rub them first, and any bad marks on. Then they used to swish it round, else do with the posser up and down, up and down. A posser was a brass round thing with holes. This thing had a handle on it, and you pressed it up and down, and there were holes in the copper plate. The ones with the three legs are the dolly pegs. You put them in and twisted. Then you emptied the dolly tub, then filled it full of clean water, and then put the clothes back in to rinse. After that you'd wring them with the mangle, and then, on a fine day, they went outside on the line. [Dolly Brassington]

Dolly tubs and peggy legs.

We had nothing at Winster. We didn't even have water on the sink, nor nothing. We used to have to go down a long way with buckets to the tap. Well, you could go on the West Bank or you could go down the gennel, and there was a tap right at the bottom, near Lyndhurst, at the bottom. We sometimes used to go up West Bank to the trough for water. There was a tap by the side where you filled your buckets. It was running into this trough all the time. There was something for the spare water to go down in. It wasn't splashing on the road. There was a continual stream of water. I don't think it was drinkable. We'd turn the tap on and got it out of that. If it was for drinking, we used about four buckets a day, because, you see, when you did your vegetables you'd got to wash them all. But when it was washday, my husband used to fill the dolly tub, and I never had to fetch any water till he came at night. It was very hard work. On washing-day, so that I didn't mess my kitchen up - because you do, don't you, when you're washing - I'd got a table mangle and used to put it outside and put the gas copper out, open the window and put a lead through it. If it was a windy day I had to get a piece of sheeting and put round it, else it would have blown the copper out - and have the dolly tub and the peggy legs, and that was my washing. [Annie Marshall]

Using a flat iron.

As for ironing, we had a special thing that dropped down from the front of the fireplace so that the iron wasn't directly up against the fire. But it would get black, so my mum used to have a sack and rub the iron on, so as to get all the bits, so as not to dirty the clothes. [Dot Fearn]

From flat irons to electric.

We had a stove in the dining room there. It was a black-leaded grate with a boiler one side and the oven the other side and the open fire in the middle with bars going across. My mother had a rack that she hooked on to the bars to heat the flat irons. You could leave it hooked on to the bars, actually, because it folded up. You could leave it there or you could move it off and put it there every time you wanted to iron. From the flat iron I progressed to a gas iron. It was very good. It had a long connecting pipe made of rubber. We had a gas tap on the wall with a nozzle on that you fitted this pipe to and just turned the tap and lit the air with a match. Then later I moved on to an electric iron. [Mildred Witham]

A rum job.

There weren't such a thing as toilet paper. You'd tear up a bit of newspaper. Your newspaper then used to be precious, because they were only a penny for your newspaper then, but still it were sort of precious. In most cases the toilets were out in the back garden - never in anybody's house, never, not even in the posh houses. When I were up at Oddo Hall - and they had three servants and the cook and that - even that hadn't got a flush toilet or anything. That was about 1922. People used to come and empty them. My dad used to do it mostly. When he finished at the quarries about dinnertime my dad would go up there, and he'd do such thing as that, like, for a bit of spare money. Only once a week. I can remember when the night-soil man used to come round. They used to come round with a cart and a tanker thing, and they used to empty these buckets into that. A rum job! [Bert Boam]

Prince and the night-soil men.

All the toilets was at the back in the gardens, but they weren't all dead level - they were regularly piggling. The toilet we had at first had a wooden seat with just one hole. Some people were lucky - they got two holes, one for children and a bigger one for adults. My dad, every Good Friday, had to empty it. We had to fetch this Izal from sanitary inspector's home before he could empty it. Later on, a few years after that, they came round for night soil, which was collected

'a wooden seat with just one hole'

about midnight. We had a dog called Prince, and that was the only time that he ever barked, when the night-soil men came, and if you were asleep the barking woke you up. I'd swear my mother said they'd done something at him, because he never barked. He was the most docile dog that I've ever known. [Gladys Hardy]

When toilets had two seats.

Everybody had an outside toilet. Our outside toilet was just a bucket with a board over and two holes in the board, and that was it until we got the water in. And then we had a water toilet, and that was outside. We had to go outside, even at night with a candle. And, if we didn't want to go out at night when we went to bed, we used to have a white enamel bucket up-stairs. My father used to mix these ashes with them that you got out of your fireplace, then you could put it on your garden. Mr Foxlow started coming round and he used to collect it. Where he took it to I don't know, unless he took it on to his fields somewhere. Before Mr Foxlow it would all have to be buried in your garden. There was no other place to put it.

I can remember the first water closet we had. We'd just got the drains in, and we had to flush it with water out of the well. The new toilet was in a different place, where they brought it closer to the house. The bucket toilets used to be nearly all at the bottom of the gardens, away, I suppose, from the smell. When we had the water toilet we brought it nearer to the back door. Before we got water in the house we used to get it out of stone troughs or out of the well and swill it with that. And that went down into the drains under the road. Outside there's a cover that says 'Frederick George Wilson', my father, and underneath that 'Builder'. That went into the central drain then. He put all his drains in first. Everybody had their own drains leading into the central drain. They had to. A lot shared, for the expense, but they shouldn't have done really - it caused a lot of trouble. I suppose today it could cause trouble – well, it does do. They don't know where half the drains are now in the village, do they?

The first water closet was when the water came into the houses, late thirties I should imagine, something like that. Then later we had a toilet with a chain. We've still got a chain out there now. How long ago would it be when we had a chain? Probably in the 1940s, after the war, I should think. [Mavis Corker]

The scavenging cart and other stories.

I was born in 1924 and lived first in Market House. There was a pot toilet but it was flushed with rainwater that we'd caught in the tank. When I was married and I lived in Woolley's Yard the toilet was right at the top of the garden. We didn't share. There were about twelve steps to climb and then a long garden path, so you had to be quick off the mark if you wanted to go quickly - you had to run, in fact. If it was a dark evening you'd have to find the matches and light the candle. We didn't actually carry a candle up the garden path. We left it in the toilet - we just took matches to light the candle.

Never remember having an earth lavatory, but some people did. The earth toilets were emptied by what we used to call the 'scavenging cart', and it used to come round every Tuesday, always at dinnertime, and fetch the buckets out of the toilets, empty them in the back of the lorry. And then the gentlemen used to sit and eat their dinner - sandwiches - and they never came, to my house anyway, to ask if they could wash their hands. Everybody round about used to close their windows and doors and not go out until they'd gone.

I think they tipped it at the bottom of Bonsall Lane. There's a little plantation there now. The kids used to play up there and get covered in it. Mrs Marshall's son was 'Jobby'. He came home one day covered, and she said, 'Tha's been on that nasty, dirty tip, where there's some nasty, dirty rats, and tha's gone and got thyself covered in jobby!' So he got the nickname of 'Jobby' Marshall and it stuck. That was Stan Marshall.

We moved from Woolley's Yard to the Bowling Green. We'd flush toilets there, both for the customers outside and for ourselves upstairs. For toilet paper we used newspaper cut up in squares and string threaded through and hung in the toilet. Every little bit of soft paper, such as Boden's bread was wrapped in lovely soft tissue paper, we used to save that, and if you had a piece of that you thought it was luxury. After that the Izal toilet paper came in, the roll. I used to think it was very slippy and shiny, and my dad said it wasn't as strong as the newspaper! If you got a piece of newspaper, you found it best to ruffle it up and make it soft. But my husband always used to say he'd rather have the Izal. He thought it was more substantial.

In the Crown I think there were two earth toilets, what I can remember, near a washhouse. Then they had water toilets put in the same yard. The toilets were very narrow. I think it was a mistake somehow, because if you were stout you had to back in, which was quite difficult in the dark. This lady from Wensley was sat on, and this other lady was in a hurry, and she backed in and sat on her. And, of course, she wasn't very pleased. She says, 'You'll have to shift. It's time to catch my bus.' Me and my friend was stood outside, and this lady from Wensley said, 'Just look at me! I'm wet through!' I says, 'And you've missed your bus!' So she had to walk back to Wensley. [Dot Fearn]

Ernest Hope remembers washday squabbles and froth on the brook.

The first piped water into Winster came from Pilsley, at the back of Birchover, and that was the first taps in Winster. Water was piped up to a reservoir at the top of West Bank, then all the taps in Winster were gravity fed, but anybody above reservoir never got the water taps. Them up at top of Bank used to have to take their water from Shothouse or else come down into Winster. They were farmers at the top of the Bank, and they'd fetch it with a horse and cart in milk churns.

A man called Herbert Boam used to fetch it in a thing like a dandy, two wheels with a 17-gallon churn, and it were pulled with a donkey. He used to stand it under spout and get some fine cloth over the top to sieve it, and then he used to bring it back to Winster and sell it one penny a bucket - just about a gallon and a half bucket, I should say.

Well, water from Birchover run 24 hours a day when weather wasn't too dry, but as soon as it came a bit of dry weather we used to be cut off, and we'd have it on about two hours in a morning and an hour at night, teatime. People used to send their buckets up in big, low lines at the side of the taps to be first to get their water the next morning, getting it in turns. There used to be as many as fifty buckets against each tap. First person got dirty water coming down the mains. Sam Hodgkinson used to turn it on and off. One day there was a man who hadn't got any. He'd been at work all day and he came back and found his wife ill, with a baby, and she'd got no water. Sam Hodgkinson had turned water off. He went up to see if he could get any, so he went and broke into the standpipe and got his own water, and he got summonsed and they sent him to Bakewell. He was found five shillings. That was a lot then. Average wages was eighteen shilling off Council, and when I first went to work at fourteen I got eight shillings a week and my keep. That was farming, and a man's wage was eighteen shillings. Same as quarrymen used to get £5 a fortnight. That was a decent wage then. School teachers used to get £2, and headmaster £5 a week.

Not everybody used the taps. People were still fetching water from down Pump Lane, and some houses on Main Street had got wells in. There was no problem with purity of the water then, only from Pump Lane. Everybody said you got diseases from the water down there. There were several cases of diphtheria about at the same time. That was when I was very small. There was one up the street, back of East Bank there. We used to run past the house because they used to fumigate it. There were two in Winster, two died with diphtheria. That would be 1927 or 1928. Some got it while the coal strike was on, General Strike.

Some people had got wells in their houses, and they fetched it from just beginning going on Birchover Lane. There was a well there. The man that let 'em have that water got summonsed for letting 'em have it. He was taken to Bakewell Court and found, because they said it wasn't fit for drinking.

Later on water was piped from Shothouse, and they had a tap at the top of Bank, and it also went to Elton at the same time. That would be about 1934,

1935. Ernest Heathcote used to own Shothouse, and he used to own the Post Office as well. He used to live at Mooresfold, but he used to run the Post Office, and the house what's at back now used to be let. As for Shothouse, it had 999 years' lease on it, and that started in about 1936. Ernest Heathcote sort of gave it to the village. And then, after 1970 time, we connected up to Ladybower. It didn't involve a lot of the roads being dug up. They just connected into the same mains.

Shothouse Spout, c. 1934, with Eric Roper (in cap)
collecting water in churns.

Where we lived on East Bank there was no water until 1950, when they did East Bank. We went outside to a tap against Walton Cottage on the grass. There were no taps inside houses until after the War, and in finish, about 1954, it were compulsory to have taps in houses. To begin with, the only ones with water were such as doctor and that, such as the Manor, big houses. It would be 1950 before they came down West Bank with water. East Bank had got no water at top end. It were about 1950 when they came down East Bank and coupled up to this other down here, and that would be the same time as the proper mains were put on.

Every Monday it was washing day in Winster, and all people had a tank of water caught from their house roofs - tank or a trough - and they used to do their washing altogether on a Monday morning. When water got short people used to get worked up, and I can remember two women fighting because one said they'd had more water than the other out of this joint trough. One of them would hit the other on the head with the ladle what she'd got water out of the trough with. That was Winster washday.

The sewerage from Winster used to go on a field down at the back of the council houses into a square big tank, and then the overflow used to go down the fields into Clough Wood Brook. On a Monday night Clough Wood Brook was covered with froth - foam from washing all running down towards the river down at Darley.

Before electric came to Winster we used to have paraffin lamps and gas lights. The gas company used to put gas into the house. They put a one-penny meter in and then you'd got a free gas stove in the house. That gas stove went with the house. If you flitted you couldn't take it with you. They used to put lead pipes round the house and gas in, burners for upstairs. Before that it used to be candles and paraffin.

A man named Crusty Bob [Hardy] used to go round with a torch on a pole, like candle tap blazing. He used to go round to light street lights as soon as it went nearly dark, and then turned them off again at ten o'clock at night. If it were moonlight there were none, they didn't used to light 'em. He got paid 10s 6d a week.

When electric came people could have it if they wanted it. It used to cost £5. They put a new line in past Winster, just east of the school, to Mill Close Mine, and then we felt we should all have electric quick, about 1932. When men were putting them poles in they used to dig hole about six foot deep, join two poles together, then get a horse, get a barb on other poles, and pull it up with that, pull it up until it was nearly straight, then five or six men hanging on ropes other side stop it going over too far. While it were like that some more men pushed soil in hole, trampled on it, and jumped on it to make it solid. These poles had a mark on where they had to be buried up to, and when they came to a piece where there were rock, instead of fetching rock off they used to saw the bottoms of the poles off, so only about a yard in ground some of them were, and they should have been six foot. But they never got blown down.

East Midlands Electricity Company wanted twelve houses to sign up for it before they put it in, so round about 1935/6 they managed to get a dozen to put it in. The ordinary people wouldn't have it in, because they said there was no heat in electric. There were oil and they had the gas light, but they were out of electric light. So it was a long while before they persuaded everybody to have it in - just after the war. They never coupled anybody up when the war was on. When the Labour Government got in they had these special cases before they could be coupled up. They wouldn't let anybody have it. It were about 1955 before they were coupling up again and let all these people have it in house. There were some without electricity and they had gas right up to 1955. They just brought the supply free to the house and put a meter in. You did the rest yourself, or get somebody else do it. There were plenty of people willing to have a go at it. All this electricity was overhead wires, and then they put them underground. Street was done first - it must have been in the '60s – and West Bank was done later, and they finished off with East Bank in the 1980s. [Ernest Hope]

Recruitment for the Great War.

I remember the first time in all my life I ever saw a moving picture. The war was on - it was the 1914 war - and at the back of the Market House they put a big sheet up, and it covered all back of the Market House. You could see soldiers marching and smoking cigarettes and that. They were wanting volunteers for army. I'd be about five then. All my life I'd always seen slides in church and so on. They used always have these lantern slides. It was marvellous to see the moving pictures! You wondered what was going off when you'd seen that, it looked so real. I think they did get quite a lot of volunteers, because there were such a lot of lads did go from Winster. [Bert Boam]

A Zeppelin over Mill Close in 1917.

The Zeppelin came over in the night. We didn't see it, but we heard it. I was brought out of bed by my mother, told to bring my clothes downstairs and get dressed and not to wake my sister. I was taken out into the front garden and I soon heard this droning sound coming from the sky in the direction of Nottingham. It came practically overhead, and there was this enormous roar. My father noticed that the lights of the mine were still blazing. They'd never been shut out, which they should have been. That started the

'a Zeppelin over Mill Close'

alert. He dashed out of the house and went down a field, the quickest way to the mine. There was a brook at the bottom and he fell in and had to be rescued. He was stuck in the brook and there was a lot of water in it. He couldn't get out as he was stuck in the slime and silt in the bottom. When mother and I found him – we had followed him – I had to go to the mine and fetch help. They told me to tell the man who was there to bring two planks and two men to lift him out. That's what happened. They pulled him out of his boots! And when they dropped him down they put him in a bed of nettles! [Harold Thomas]

Memories of the First World War.

First of all, I'm not a Winster person. I was born in Youlgreave in 1913 and came off a large family. I was ninth in the row of twelve. My parents weren't very well off and during the First World War, which I remember very slightly, we were on rations. I can just remember my mother saying, 'This is your ration', which was about two ounces of sugar in a little blue bag. One day during the war a brother of mine, who had been fighting on the Somme, came on leave. I remember he went back and he hadn't been back long before he was killed. Eighty years later I went to visit the place where he was killed. I thought he'd got a tombstone up, but when I got there all there was was his name on the wall among thousands of other names. [Bill Slaney]

Evacuees from Manchester.

My long association with Winster started on the 1st of September 1939, when I, along with thousands of children, were evacuated. There were about a hundred of us from Cavendish Road School in Withington, which is a suburb of Manchester. We were put on a bus with luggage labels tied to our coats, name and home address on it. I had a little rucksack with one or two belongings in. The buses were driven to a railway station and we got aboard a train. Our parents weren't with us. We'd had to leave them at the school, and we just didn't know where we were going. I was too young, really. I was five-and-a half at the time. Well, the teachers, or the carers, entertained us on this train journey. We had to go to sleep when we went through a tunnel and open our eyes when we came out of the tunnel.

I can't remember any of the teachers on that journey. I just remember lots of children and being on a train and then being put on a bus and arriving at what I now know as the Burton Institute. There were tables set out for us to eat. We had sandwiches packed up with us, and I'd been told not to eat mine until I was told to. Other children on the bus or train had eaten theirs, and when we got to the tables at Winster I was eating mine and wouldn't share. I must have been a horrible child! I told them they shouldn't have eaten theirs on the train. The tables were cleared away and the billeting process started.

Nobody knew who I was. I don't know why nobody knew. Maybe I was one of the younger ones that hadn't had a carer with them. Some of

'evacuees from Manchester'

the mothers had come, but my mum didn't. I remember a table on the platform, and the person there had lists of names, and they were saying, 'Who's she with?' But I wasn't with anybody. 'Well, who are we going to put her with?' I remember running to this lady and saying, 'Please can I be your little girl?' She patted me on the head and said, 'Well, I'm very sorry, I can't.' I now know that the reason was she was very heavily pregnant. This was Mrs Fairey, and she was expecting Barry.

So I turned from Mrs Fairey and ran again and put my arms round another lady and said, 'Please can I be your little girl? Will you be my mummy?' I'd obviously been told by my mother that I was to have a new mummy and daddy. This lady had gone purely and simply to help. She hadn't been married too long - four or five years - and she had no children of her own. She lived in a little cottage, and, as it happened, she'd got a spare bed. She lived at Pembroke House [now Brae Cottage] on East Bank. The only reason she had a bed was because her cousin had been up from London for a holiday, along with a couple of aunts and uncles, and they'd all gone scurrying back off to London when this war panic started. So this lady, who I called mummy, took me to her mother's, at Jasmine Cottage on East Bank. There I met the dog Pip and was made welcome. Pip and I were the best of friends right up to him going. [Muriel Gould]

'A bit more streetwise'.

The councillors came round, and you had to say whether you would have a boy or girl, one or two. Then people in the Burton Institute sorted them and brought them to the houses where they were to stay, and took the address so that the addresses could be sent back to the parents in Manchester. They'd all got their names pinned to them, and they had their gas masks. They'd only got little suit-cases, tiny little cases, as they'd brought very little with them - perhaps one set of clothes or pyjamas or something like that.

They were different from us. They seemed a bit more - as we would say now - streetwise. They brought their own teachers, because between forty and fifty, I should think, came. Our school obviously wasn't big enough for everybody, so at the first we went mornings and they went afternoons, and the following week they went mornings and we went afternoons. We used the Burton Institute for communal lessons - sewing, knitting and things like that. [Eileen Crowder]

'Some couldn't settle'.

We had a lot of evacuees come into the village, and we had quite a number at Vernon House. First of all we started off with three girls, and then the whole family came. They stayed for what seemed a long time, really. They came from Manchester. There wasn't a teacher for them at Winster School to begin with, but one came much later from Stanton who stayed at Vernon House - Mrs

> Winster Wisdom: 'Never run after a bus once you've caught it.'

Monkhouse. Well, we could only get to school half a day. It was very different in those days. Eventually it sorted itself out. A lot of evacuees came, but quite a number of them couldn't settle and went back. One, Muriel, stayed with Mrs Gregory for many, many years. She was a daughter to them. She was a lovely girl. [Marion Drinkall]

For some it was too much.

Geoffrey Swarbrick and his brother lived at the Shoulder of Mutton, on the West Bank. I remember a story about those little boys, which was very sad, really, poor little things. The train came to Darley Dale railway station from Manchester. Well, this little boy decided he wanted to go to his mummy, so he got his brother and took him down on the track. They somehow found the railway line, and they were missing for quite a while, and everyone was up in arms in the village. In a village there's possibly a lot of gossip, but deep down I think people love each other and everyone is concerned. If one is ill, everyone is concerned, and everyone was concerned for these two little boys when we heard they had run away. The police eventually caught them walking up the railway lines trying to get home. I think the parents kept them at home after that. [Amy Slater]

Billeted at Winster Hall.

We had the Royal Army Service Corps billeted at the Hall, but the men only stayed there for a fortnight. Then they went to Tansley for another week and then they were posted abroad. They were very young men at the beginning of their service. The Hall was used afterwards as a factory, where they made pokers and hearth-tidies and things like that. That employed a lot of women. [Dot Fearn]

Bombing.

I suppose we were aware of the war with the evacuees coming, and then, later on, a landmine dropped near Cratcliffe and another one down near Via Gellia. I remember vividly the night that Sheffield was bombed, because we were taken up to the top of the Bank up near the Rock Field, so we got a really good view of right over, and the whole of the skyline was bright red. I shall never forget it, and you could hear planes going over all the time. It's just something that stuck in your memory.

Another thing, dad was working at Rolls Royce. He lodged there, and the lady he stayed with had to go away to look after her mother. So mum took us two to look after dad and Mr Bass, who was the landlady's husband, and that was the time when Derby was bombed. We arrived there to find that the air-raid shelter had just been newly concreted, so we couldn't go in it. We went in the kitchen and built the fire up, and we sat there in the firelight, and mum read to us while the bombing was going off. The next day, no water anywhere, so big containers came in the streets. We went off with buckets and the local people of Derby couldn't understand why we were not spilling any of our water. Our pails were full to the brim, but, of course, we were used to carrying water at

Winster, and they in Derby were not. So we got home with full pails. Coming home on the train we had to get special tickets to get on to the station, because the station had been badly bombed at Derby, so we saw the damage there on our way back to Winster. [Eileen Crowder]

Frightened by bombs.

It was in the war, about 1940 or '41, when bombing was at its worst. They dropped a landmine and a load of incendiary bombs in Youlgreave. They were after the Battery works in Bakewell, but they got the wrong valley. It lit up like day here in Winster. Well, Taffy, the Bateman's horse, was in a field above East Bank, and it frightened him, and he went running round and round field. There were soldiers billeted in Winster Hall at this time. They'd been fetching firewood from round about, and they'd taken wood from off top of mine which was meant to stop you falling down. So Taffy went running round and fell down mine. Joe Banks were a miner. He went down to have a look at him, but he were dead. So he put some lime on him. [Ernest Hope]

Bert and Dorothy Bateman at Bank Top c.1940 with Taffy,
the horse that was frightened by bombs and fell down a mine shaft.

A Prisoner of War.

In May 1940 I was captured at Dunkirk. I went out there in January, and I'd only been in the army since December. I saw the last boat go out at Dunkirk. There were not many of us left, goodness knows. I saw them go off. I had a pal not so long since told me that he saw me when I was standing guiding the troops on the ship, like. I think they were about dead, because we'd done a bit of fighting. I was captured and marched down 200 miles, and I ended up in Trier in Germany, near Luxembourg. We slept in fields, and all that, and we were treated very bad. There were children spitting on us, and so on. My first capture was the 25th May. I escaped the first time, pinched a motorbike and off I went, but I got captured again. The second spell lasted till the end of the war. We were freed by General Patton himself coming through. It was dead on five years, right from leaving Dunkirk. I was in Munich listening to Churchill on the 9th May 1945. We heard that Patton was holding back from bombing Munich until we'd got out and away from there. When we got to England we had to go to a rehabilitation camp. We were marched there by Redcaps with alsatians, and we were there for three days while they washed us down and dressed us. They closed the railway for all prisoners to come upwards to Derby. We'd never seen money. We'd never seen anything. We were dumbed and excited and crying. There were a lad went up further to Buxton to change for somewhere, and we clung together like two sardines, and at Derby we said our good-byes, because I got off at Matlock. I landed at ten o'clock at night, and I sat on the causeway. We hadn't heard from home for six months. I'd sent letters, but we'd been on the march since January 20th. A woman who lived in the chip shop in Matlock shouted in street, 'It's Harold Barnsley!' And she said, 'Come on, I'll take you to see Edith [Harold's fiancée].' I said, 'Alright...' She come to the door and said, 'Eh, it's Harold is it?' She was waiting for me, and that was the beginning of a life again. You do understand, the situation would seem nothing. We didn't see anything - potato fields, mountains in mid-winter. We dug a hole to sleep in. You were as hard as nuts - you had to be. It was late, so I stayed at Edith's and came up to Winster next morning. She came with me in a taxi, and I'd never seen so many tears in all our lives! She'd waited for me, and after that she was told that she couldn't have any time off. A London company had come up and took over Paton and Baldwin's, where she'd worked. The only way you could have time off was to marry. She'd waited for me and I'd come back, and we were happy. We were married in May 1946. My dad said, 'What are you going to do? You're not leaving Winster, are you? I'll find thee a house in Winster.' And he took me round the corner and there was this old cottage [Stepney House]. I bought it for £10 and did it up with about £250, which was what was left from the money I'd been paid – five years' wages. So that's how I landed up back in Winster. [Harold Barnsley]

Giving thanks for the end of the war.

A lady called Bessie Boden, who was our Sunday School teacher, found this lovely duet 'O Lovely Peace' and taught it to me and Jean. So really and truly Bessie started us singing. It all stems back to Bessie.

[Amy sings]
'Oh lovely peace with plenty crowned,
Oh lovely, lovely peace,
Come spread thy blessings, thy blessings all around...'

...and, of course, contralto takes the lead there. At the end of the war I can remember that Jean and I had been asked to sing in Birchover. And my father said, 'Oh, you must sing 'Oh lovely Peace'.' And it was so appropriate. [Amy Slater]

Milan Prokop leaves Czechoslovakia for Winster.

Under the German occupation we weren't allowed to find the jobs we would have liked, or go to schools or universities. That was reserved for Germans only. So I had to learn to be an electrical engineer, as opposed to going into the army or the air force. I would have gone into the air force, had conditions been normal. Under German occupation I managed to finish in a labour camp in 1944, and I stayed there until 1945 when we were liberated.

While I was in the camp we had seen trains. It was 1944-45. We had seen open trains with quite a few dead bodies, and some people were standing. They had on a pyjama type of uniform. They were being transported to concentration camps in wintertime. The clothing they had on was very thin, so many just froze in the open carriages. That's something I've just remembered.

In 1945 the Communists came to power. I couldn't understand why Czechoslovaks would take their side, against their own people, after the treatment that we had endured under the Germans. So I left Czechoslovakia. We had no passports, so I travelled by train to the Austrian border and with another man walked across to Vienna. It could have been 80 miles or so. This was the beginning of my journey to England. The part of Vienna that we were in came under Russian rule, and there were checkpoints all over the place. There were quite a few of us by that time, from many nationalities, and we contacted a group of people on the railway station in Vienna who could help us to escape. We got on to a train with a guide, but when we left the train we ran into a Russian patrol. If they had caught us, we would have finished back in Czechoslovakia, or perhaps in the Soviet Union. So we ran in all directions and walked through the night till we reached Linz. There we decided to register with the Americans. The officer advised me to go to one of the camps on the outside of the town. We stayed there for a few months, waiting for work, because there were countries from all over the world which were short of men.

I had a letter from a Czech who was a priest. He came from the same place as I did. My father was in the army, and later on he was in the Customs and Excise. My parents, who knew he was coming to Austria, asked him to communicate with me, so he gave me their message. The news was that they had had a 'funeral' for me at home. I've wondered ever since then, you know, how my father or his friends had been able to arrange my 'funeral' and say that I had died. They must have worked with doctors and JPs and various other people in authority, in order to get away with this. So I was 'buried'.

Later, when I returned to Czechoslovakia in 1991, for the first time since 1948, my sister said that after I had left, my father had lost his job. He had to do manual work, and the family were ostracised. I wonder what happened after my funeral, whether the authorities found out that I wasn't in the coffin or whether somebody denounced my father. I don't think he could have been denounced, because I think he would have been imprisoned. It is a mysterious situation that I still can't understand.

We applied to work in England, and were transported to Münster in Germany, and to Rotterdam, and by ship to Harwich. That was my first experience of a sea voyage. I still remember it [Milan laughs], obviously seasick! Oh dear! And I wasn't the only one! Then we travelled to London by train, and from there to an old air force camp in Shropshire, not far from Market Drayton. The camp was called Child's Ercal. I can remember spending time doing nothing – waiting, being bored, wondering what had happened at home and how long it would be before the war started again. We were still planning to join the air force or the army, as we believed that the war could begin again at any time, because the situation between East and West was so strained. But war didn't break out.

Whilst we were in the camp at Market Drayton we had a choice of where we might apply. There were applications for workers in coalmines and on the farms. Then requests for workers for a brick factory came, and we thought a brick factory would be a well paid job. The factory was at Friden, five miles from Winster on the way to Buxton. We thought the job would last only a few months and then we would join the air force or the army.

Winster Hall housed perhaps 40 or 45 of us. We arrived by train at Darley Dale, and we were transported by coaches to Winster. We thought it was odd that there was nobody around. I stayed in one of the three wooden outbuildings, which, when you face the Hall, were to the left of the main building. I know there was a passage from one end of the building to the far end, but I cannot remember how many rooms there were. There was a fairly large room with a stove. We very rarely had coal for the stove in those days, so we were forever cold. There must have been about fifty people altogether, and twenty stayed in the main building of the Hall.

On a typical day at the brick factory we were driven to work in coaches. It was Silver Service in those days. I remember one of the drivers, a Mr Allen. There were about three coaches full of people - not only from Winster, but also from Elton and Youlgreave. Friden was the major employer of men in those day, although a large proportion of people from Winster worked at Enthoven's [lead smelters]. We started work at eight o'clock and finished at half-past-four. We were given breakfast before leaving. It was completely different from the food we were used to. Cornflakes! We hadn't seen Cornflakes or Weetabix before, and people grumbled. I shall always remember beetroot sandwiches, because it was something unusual, something I wouldn't have thought existed! And at the end of the day we would go back to Winster - and be bored! What to do with ourselves again?

---

*Winster Wisdom: 'It isn't the early riser:
it's the well spender of the day.'*

At the factory I started by making bricks of various types. We had to load wheelbarrows with sand and push the wheelbarrows to the machines, where local people were operating the machines. It was heavy work. We had a break at mid-day. After a few months I started shift-work on the kilns, so it meant travelling there and back on a pushbike - there weren't any convenient buses. The trip every day, there and back, was ten miles. When you did this sort of work you were in good condition, what with the work and pushbiking up hill and down dale - and always the wind against you!

It was in 1949 or 1950 when people started leaving Winster and the brick factory for other places. Most from the Hall who came here from the continent as refugees went to Derby, Wolverhampton or Birmingham. A few of us stayed. I met my future wife in Winster and we got married in 1950.

I married Brenda Hawksworth. Her family used to have a shop in the Main Street, at the bottom of West Bank. I found it difficult to mix with the local people. Firstly, I couldn't speak English. I don't think I even knew how to say, 'Good morning!' Then we were told by one of the men who came in 1947 that people were discussing before Christmas whether they should invite us to their homes. They decided not to. The reason was because of the shortage of food, I suppose. Everybody from the continent felt that we were not wanted here because we were foreigners. Perhaps all rural communities, not only Winster, feel uncomfortable with anything new or different. In those days if you travelled from Winster to Elton it was a great event. People used to walk. There were very few cars, some motorbikes, but mainly pushbikes. I don't know whether the local people resented us.

So here I am in Winster without any English and I meet Brenda. I don't think it was my dashing good looks that first attracted her! On my part, it was attraction at first sight. We met when she used to go from the Main Street, from their house, to a farm on the top of West Bank for milk, and I used to go for walks. I think by that time I knew how to say 'Hello.' It was 1949, and I must have had a few words of English. We started going out and then I started going to their house. Brenda's mother died in the autumn of 1949 and we got married the following January.

When I came to Winster I was very glad to leave all the troubles behind. Winster was a peaceful place. I now had a stable home where I could relax and not expect trouble all the time. When I saw the countryside for the first time, when we were out at Darley Dale, I thought, what a pretty place this is. You know, I still think so.

So we got married in 1950 and moved to Grimsby, where Brenda had some relations. I went to the Labour Exchange to enquire about the labour situation there. They said they couldn't do anything for me, because I lived in Derbyshire, but, if I lived in Grimsby, they could find me work. So we returned to Winster. Before we came back I had to register. In those days everywhere I went I had to register. If I stayed in one place for three days I had to register with the police.

We came to Winster and I found work - I believe it was the following day - back at Friden. That was the last place I wanted to see! So I went to the police station in Matlock and told this story that we had come from Grimsby a couple of days ago, and registered. I remember this man saying, 'Why didn't you register on your first day?' He said, 'If you don't behave, we will send you back where you came from.' So when I got back to Winster, my wife could see I was upset, and I told her what had happened at the police station. She phoned and spoke to the sergeant and explained to him what the policeman had told me. The sergeant said, 'The policeman said that in jest!' It was a bad joke. Not exactly a welcoming situation! Back to normal life here again.

I left Friden after a few years and I started driving long-distance lorries till 1957, and then we moved to Canada. The wife couldn't get used to the life over there, so after five years we came back to Winster again. I went to the Labour Exchange in Matlock. 'Why did you come here? Why didn't you go somewhere else? We've a shortage of work here.' I said to this man, 'Because my wife comes from here and we used to live here.' 'There's not enough work for you. Why did you come here in the first place?' I'd had different treatment over in Canada. There I got on with the work and I felt a human being again. But coming back here I flew off the handle after hearing this man, and I told him what I thought. Mr Buckley, who was in charge of the Labour Exchange, came out of the office and I told him what happened. He asked me to go to the office. He remembered me from before. We talked things over. This other man - I don't know whether he lost his job or if he was transferred, but I didn't see him again. I started working on the railway in Darley Dale.

In those days that was the main line that went to Manchester. I worked there from the autumn of 1962 till 1964. Then they started closing different railway stations and I was out of work. They said to me, 'You know, if you were British you would have been kept on and you would have been helped to find a job at a different location. But because you haven't British nationality, we can't do anything to help you. So I left in the summer of '64 and started work at D. P. Battery at Bakewell, and I stayed there till 1970, till the place closed down. I was then out of work for a year. What I found out later on, before the place closed down, is that local people were helped by the management to find different jobs. I didn't know about that till about two years later when I talked to various people. So I was roaming around the district, always going to the same places asking for work. Then I started working at Cintride in Bakewell. That was abrasives - abrasive sanding discs and sheets. I made masonry drills, drills for steel - this type of thing. Then I had trouble with my health in 1985 and I haven't been able to work since. I was never able to use my skills as an electrical engineer, because I wasn't allowed to. I remember going to the Post Office in Matlock for a job when the Battery closed in 1970. But they said, 'No job,' and after that it was a closed shop.

It'll be four years tomorrow when Brenda was cremated. Brenda died of cancer in 1993. First she fell over Bertie, our dog, and broke her leg, and while she was in hospital they X-rayed her and found that she had cancer on her lungs. They gave her a year-and-a-half to live. They put a pin in her broken thigh bone. She was getting on nicely. She was short of blood, too. She was given four or five pints of blood. About two weeks after her fall I hadn't seen Brenda look so well, thinking back, for quite a few years. Having extra blood, a full supplement of blood, made all the difference. She looked so well. She started walking around in the hospital with a Zimmer frame, and .... I'm not going to talk about it.

I have had happy times with Brenda, most of the time. Sometimes, as with everybody, there was friction. A lot of the friction was caused by others who spoke to Brenda. They told Brenda what they thought about me or what they had heard about me. Brenda repeated it to me. I said to her on quite a few occasions, 'How can they say anything about me if they don't know me?' I used to work at Enthoven when I left the brick factory. This type of work - at the brick factory and at Enthoven - was a type of work I wasn't used to. Before I came here I never dreamt I'd do this type of work. I was not able to speak English, so either people said I was snobbish or that I didn't want to have anything to do with them. It wasn't the case. I just couldn't talk English. I couldn't speak English as well as I would have liked.

I haven't talked about such things, even to Brenda. I don't know why not. I don't know whether it was because I didn't want to rake the ashes or I thought she wouldn't be interested. Or is it a throwback to the time when I was young and we had to watch everything we said, because of the Germans or the Communists? You had to be very careful what you said. So you are the first person to whom I've mentioned anything about my life.

I still keep thinking about those beetroot sandwiches - every so often! [Milan laughs] [Milan Prokop]

Louis Vincent leaves Yugoslavia for Winster.

I was born in ex-Yugoslavia. Times were hard. We were very poor. My parents had a smallholding. You started school when you were eight. So I started in 1938, but I finished in 1940, more or less, because during the war soldiers were in the school. Then Tito's underground organisation started blowing the railways up, doing damage, so we got penalised. People were hung round the railways - six or seven people. This happened in 1943 or 1944, and then later on they took 211 or 212 people into concentration camps. So it wasn't very good. My mum's side of the family were affected. Her brother died in a concentration camp. On my dad's side three brothers died in concentration camps. We were classed as Slovaks at that time. Because we wasn't Croatian people, we were treated differently. It became Croatia in 1940. Up to then we had Slovak people, Czechs, Ukrainians, Italians, Germans, Polish, Russians - all sorts, living together in harmony.

After the war there was nothing in Yugoslavia. There were no factories. There was just smallholdings, villages. I went on an apprenticeship scheme to Czechoslovakia, to Bratislava, to learn to be an electrician. I did nearly three years. Czechoslovakia and Yugoslavia had a good sort of partnership, but when the Communists took over we were forced to work and on Sundays. They tried to ban you from going to the Catholic Church, forced you to work, and then on Monday it was in the papers that you had volunteered! We were living in this

Winster Hall in the 1950s. Mr Denham (seated)
had a shop on Main Street [now Beech View].

big hostel. If you didn't go to work, you didn't get your food, so you have to go to survive. And then on Monday, in every paper, it said that you had volunteered! You had done it with pleasure! So we were put to work on the railway, cleaning. Because I was an electrician, I were cleaning all the switches! Others were sweeping the streets, and they said, 'Oh, do it freely for the country.' That's how it was.

I decided to run away. A relative and his wife was living with us. He had previously been arrested, because he had spoken out openly. He was in jail about twelve months. So when he came out of prison we just decided, 'That's enough!' The first attempt was with five friends. We scarpered to Austria, over the border, but the Austrian Police caught us and sent us back, because they said we were under age as refugees, or displaced persons. But the next time, with my relatives, we managed to get through. When I finally escaped I was eighteen.

I was travelling with my friend, my niece and their baby, who we pushed in a pram. We escaped from Bratislava and went from Slovakia to Czech Republic. We went towards the Austrian border as quickly as possible, and that's where we made a plan. The plan was to escape through the fields. Can you imagine pushing a little pram - not a fancy pram but an old-fashioned one - through the ploughed fields? We were pulling and pushing. When we escaped to the other side they actually fired, but we were too far in the Austrian fields by then.

When we got to Austria we arrived in the Russian zone, instead of the British, American or French. Linz was one part Russian, and one part was what they called International Western Powers. We crossed the Danube on an inner tube - like a tractor or a car inner tube. We put the pram on that and paddled across to the other side. We were scared that we'd get caught, so earlier my friend had made us documents, but we couldn't read them as they were in German. As we didn't get caught we tore them up. They were just in case the police caught us. When we got to Linz we met someone who gave us an idea of where to go. He'd helped people before, you see, and he told us where to register as displaced persons. So that's what we did.

The camp was run by British and Americans. When we got there I met a bloke from Bratislava, from Czechoslovakia, and it were Leslie [Früwald], and we've been together ever since. This was Leslie who married Betty Burton. I recognised him because I'd seen him in Bratislava swimming baths. He's a very good swimmer. We used to pass comments on how good he was. I said, 'Oh what are you doing here?' After that we were friends ever after, like brothers.

I think we were in the camp for about six or seven weeks. It were hard. There were very poor food. They asked us to go and help in the kitchen, so you got a bit more. The British and American soldiers were very kind. They give us extra bread or something, so we more or less volunteered to do that. We went helping farmers as well, when they let us out of the camp. The farmers didn't pay us, but now and again they gave us a shilling or two, Austrian money. We couldn't spend it, because we didn't know the value then until we learned a little bit more. After that things improved a little food-wise, and there were a lot of older people in the camp, weaving baskets from cane and selling them, so they could buy something, because we were rationed. A slice of bread - that's what you got - or turnip soup. If you found a piece of meat, you were lucky. But we actually managed to improve our standard by volunteering to do a bit of work to buy a bit of bread, about a shilling. As far as we were concerned (me and Leslie), we got on very well.

There's a rumour in Winster that Leslie and I actually escaped by swimming the Danube, which isn't quite true. But we did actually get to swim the Danube. It was a nice warm day. We said, 'Let's have a swim in the Danube.' He were a marvellous swimmer. He swam the distance in no time, but I gradually got more or less stuck with the current, and, instead of finishing up straight across, I were about half a kilometre down river and actually landed in the Russian zone again. I had to get back again, quick! I managed to get back to the other side again, but I was struggling now. He was brilliant. He were shouting and giving me encouragement. There was one stage when I thought I was going to drown, because I didn't have enough power left and the current was taking me. He said, 'Swim with the current and not against it.' So he helped me a bit.

Whilst we were in Linz, notices started coming to the camp from other countries to apply for work. Well, we put in for every country, more or less - whichever one come first. Then they announced that Great Britain was taking people as coalminers, or you could volunteer for the army. So that's what we did. When we were accepted, we had an examination again. They moved us from Linz to Münster in Germany, where we had more medicals. We were in quarantine for seven days. We couldn't go out of camp or anywhere, because you had to have an injection every 24 hours against infectious diseases. Then the cleaners there disinfected us as well. It was quite humiliating really. We had one examination after another, completely starkers. You had to strip off and move through, and there were - what you call? - 'sex' people. There was a German lady doctor to examine you. We were terrified! Your private parts! Some men actually went with ladies, and they had caught sexual diseases, but we'd never tried anything like that, so we went to the UK.

We arrived at Harwich, and from there we travelled to London, and then to a camp in Market Drayton, Shropshire. The food was very good. We weren't used to it, but we appreciated it. There were loudspeakers in different languages to tell us what to do - when to go for breakfast and dinner in the canteen. It was announced on the loudspeaker that a bricks work in Derbyshire required people, so we volunteered. Two days later they took us to the station and sent us on a train to Darley Dale, where a lorry was waiting for us and brought us to Winster Hall.

We felt happy, because we thought, 'This is the start. We are going to work and earn money in order to get on.' And that is what we did. We was quite content, really, to get a job, because from the beginning, in Linz and then in Germany, you were a Nobody. We thought this would give us a chance to be Someone, to start a new life, and that is what happened.

We couldn't speak any English whatsoever. That was our biggest problem. As far as I can remember there were round about forty of us, of different nationalities, who came to work at Friden. There were Bavarians, Austrian, Polish, Ukrainians, Russian and about seven Hungarian people. Each nationality seemed to keep themselves to themselves

They welcomed us as we got off the lorry. We had our names on labels. I've still got mine somewhere. We had to go in as our names were called, and they showed us the rooms. Outside, where that big tree is, there was a sort of veranda. A bit further back there were two huts that they had used during the war for the Army, and that's when me and Leslie found our friendship was made stronger. There were showers, bathroom and toilet. We really liked it. There were two sleeping in each room. There was a sort of resting room where you had chairs, a radio, a sofa and a stove for heating. And there was a sort of boiler, so the pipes came all around your bedroom. As far as I remember, there were four or five bedrooms. Others lived upstairs in the Hall. Downstairs there was a billiard room, recreation room, dining room and kitchen. We ate in the canteen in

Winster Wisdom: 'Sup, and sup hearty!'

the Hall. They provided good meals, actually, because everything was still on ration. When we first arrived the WVS welcomed us with a party. It was very nice, but we couldn't understand much because of the language. We played games like Postman's Knock, behind the door. They gave you a name and if they shouted you, you went to the other side of the door and had a kiss - just one or two! We had a bit of a dance. It was just hopeless, because we couldn't speak, that was the problem. But we learned quickly.

When we started work we had to have a week in hand before we were paid. We had no money, but as soon as we were paid we went to Matlock on the bus and bought a Czech Slovak/English dictionary. We started learning from that. In the meantime, in the process of trying to educate us into the English language, the schoolmaster at Winster School had opened a night-class, but I only went twice. We thought he was learning us proper English! Although we tried, the spelling was just too much. We found that listening was the way to learn quicker. The first words you learned were swear words, because at work that was the way. From our book we learnt the words for things we wanted to buy. Once we had no handkerchiefs – there were no paper tissues in them days – so we learnt this word 'handkerchief, handkerchief, handkerchief' to go across to the Post Office. The lady in the Post Office then was Mrs Spencer, and I remember walking across, opening the door, going in... We'd forgotten! We stood there just like pillocks, honestly. In the end - this was the breakthrough - I put my hand in my pocket, brought it out and went 'sniff, sniff,' and she brought out a box of handkerchiefs. We bought two or three boxes each. Then we went to pictures with our money, and actually both of us started courting a girl in Matlock, but it didn't last, because we couldn't stay and talk properly. We didn't even go to the pub, because we didn't know how to ask for a drink. Eventually, though, we did. Across the road from Winster Hall was a pub named the Crown, and it would be about five or six weeks later when we first made an attempt. Others had tried before us. I think this was the first time we ever had English beer. I didn't like it. I don't think either of us did. It's an acquired taste, I think. I found English beer sort of sweet and very dark. We was trying to mix our drinks, and if there was any girl standing nearby, we'd be there!

The ladies of the Women's Institute put on a show and a dance in Winster, and we were invited free of charge. That was where I met Eunice, and that was it. That's when I really started learning English. When I began courting she intro-duced me to the family, and I started picking it up. School classes were still going on, but I went to Eunice's family. There were two brothers at home, and one was coming up to grammar school, and he give me the better learning. It was a good incentive to speak English. Eunice had a baby of three years of age when I met her, and they were buying the child comics. I picked one up, and the pictures and the writing underneath made the meaning stick in your head. A good way of learning, the same as children just starting school.

At work the biggest problem was the language. Walter Terenzu was a Ukrai-nian, already in Friden, and he was our spokesman. He remained in Winster and he and his wife now live in the Manor. I got a job to make bricks by hand, special bricks. Machines couldn't do it, but we did. But because I wasn't twenty-one they wouldn't pay me the full wage, because at that time there was a law that you couldn't get full money until you were twenty-one. After a week of learning I was doing the same amount of bricks as the others. They said, 'Now you are on piece-work.' There was a foreman on the job and he said the following week that I was good enough. So I do it, and there have to be seventy bricks. If you made seventy you were top grade. I got used to it, and I could make double the amount, but the foreman wouldn't let me, because I wouldn't get paid. There was a bit of discrepancy there, because I were getting better results than he was, and he were supposed to be master of the job. But it seemed to me that he was sort of playing with me. Leslie got his job in the sand shed, wheeling wheelbarrows full of sand into a great big machine that was grinding it to dust. So I was better off than he was, because there was no dust where I was, but the money wasn't really big. I think we worked eight hours a day, and on Saturday until dinnertime. When we came back to the Hall we had a wash and a meal. Sometimes, if the meal was ready, you didn't have a chance to have a wash and shave.

There was a foreman who was overall in charge, and he met Eunice's mother in the pictures at Matlock and told her that I was not a very good bloke. So she told me, 'That's it, don't come any more.' But we were stuck in love and we just carried on. I went back again into the house and the old lady had to give in, because she was a widow.

There was once a misunderstanding. We thought the people in the Hall were giving us grass to eat. That came about because they give us sandwiches to take to work. This particular time we got these sandwiches and they were water-cress. We hadn't seen watercress before, and when we opened the sandwiches at dinnertime we thought, Oh, they're feeding us on grass, and we didn't like it, so we got Walter, our spokesman, to go and see Mr Burston the manager. He was an ex-naval officer, living at Stanton House, on West Bank, opposite where Dr Fletcher lived. Walter tried to tell him, so after we finished work he came to Winster Hall and gave us a speech saying that it wouldn't happen again. So we didn't have any more watercress sandwiches. Later, we saw other people eating it, so we didn't worry. Mr Burston was very understanding.

Now, in the meantime, he asked if anybody wanted to go for shift work on the kilns. I volunteered for that, because there was more money, as you worked more hours. So I worked seven days a week. There were no breaks. That's because I wanted to get married. I married on 28th May 1949 at Bakewell, and I was at Friden on the kilns until 1951, after which I left. We had a contract with Friden for three years until 1951, and we couldn't move before then. If you moved you had to report to the police. When I first married and lived in Elton, I had to report to the police that I had moved from Winster Hall. When I returned from Elton [5 November 1949] to live in this cottage, I had to report that I was back in Winster, on East Bank. We acquired this cottage through Mr Burton, who had a shop on Main Street. He were delivering the groceries to Eunice's mam. Eunice's mam wasn't very well, and she developed Parkinson's disease. During her illness she actually called me a foreign bastard. But I wasn't to give up. In the end Mr Burton could see what was causing the tension, and we were glad to move anywhere. We had put our name down for a council house, but he said, 'There's a cottage, but it wants doing up. It has been condemned.' It belonged to Mrs Greatorex, who lived next door, and was to be sold at auction. When the bloke who intended buying it found out that it was condemned, he declined, he wouldn't have it, so that's when I got a chance with Mr Burton, who said, 'How much?' It were fifty quid! But fifty pounds! Where do we get fifty quid from? So Eunice's brother give us the deposit of twenty-five pounds, and then we paid every week a £1 until it was paid off. Owing to the papers, you know, the changeover, it cost altogether £75. That was turnover, papers and everything. So we got a good bargain.

A friend of Eunice's flitted us over one evening. But we had nothing. Just before we married people had given us a bit of money and I think there was a few pounds. We had to buy forks and knives so we have something to eat with. We went on honeymoon to Matlock Bath on a bicycle. Eventually we bought a wardrobe. That's how we started. I was quite domesticated, because we had to do our own washing and look after ourselves when we were in the Hall.

The village people were quite kind to us, but there was much more animosity between the people within the Hall itself. For example, some of the Russians disagreed politically with the Czechs, and some of the Czechs didn't agree with the Slovaks. Twice we had to stop fighting developing. If you had applied for British nationality, you had to have a clean record. If you did anything wrong, you wouldn't get it. When we first arrived in the Hall we were sat down, like in a seminar, and told 'These are the rules, and, if you don't obey or you misbehave, this is what will happen.' You had to behave. There was a Russian expelled from Britain altogether because of his behaviour. So we were very, very careful.

Once I had a fight at Friden. When we were working on the kilns we used the canteen. If you paid for a proper meal, it was 1s, or whatever. We took sandwiches, because it was cheaper, and went to the canteen for a jug of tea, which we took back to the works, where we had a table with seating. Someone always put salt in your cup of tea, just for devilment, but it were getting beyond a joke. Every time you had a drink you had to spit it out because it was horrible. This particular time I waited and I done it to him. He was a boiler man. When he tasted it - same thing - he spat it out. He got hold of me and started hitting me in the lips, but I'd got my hands round his neck and I held on, because I'm not very big. I held on tight and tighter, until he come down to the floor. Then the foreman come through and broke us up. But the boilerman was the start of it. He got the lecture, not me. This had been going on for a long time. He was actually against the foreigners. But that was only once, never no more.

The only person in the Hall who sometimes stepped out of line was Zakić, and we had to keep an eye on him. There was a dance in the Burton Institute almost every weekend. In a continental way the girls were one side and the boys on the other side of the Hall. We bowed to a girl and then, if she accepted, we had a dance with her. Zakić went and they ignored him. They actually laughed at him, and he went berserk. It started there, but we managed to get him out. But he was going to do somebody! The English blokes came and they were dancing with the English girl, you see. We restrained him, we had a good talk to him, and he calmed down.

I worked at Enthoven's after my contract expired at Friden. When I first started they were smelting all the lead - not the lead ore, but lead waste - from other factories where they made batteries - old batteries and waste lead pipes, all that sort of thing. It was all recycling of waste. After a few months of being on these fires they made a big new smelting furnace, so I was promoted to a better job. It was the best paid job around this district in Derbyshire, because the lead industry was better paid than any other. Eventually I got lead poisoning. In them days nobody knew that lead was causing the illness. The new ideas were there. They told you to wear gloves, which were supplied, protective clothing, overalls, and that sort of thing. That were all there. But you didn't change your shoes, and you come home in the boots that you were working in. Eventually they changed all that. It was in the 1970s, when people starting developing illnesses, that they started to look at the situation, and eventually the ministry people came and took a sample of blood from us, and I was sent home the same day. They found out that I had too much lead in me – 190mg. Every human being has got lead in them, but it averages around 70 to 80mg. Working in the lead industry it is acceptable up to 80mg, but above that it is dangerous. Altogether I worked at Enthoven's for 23 years. When they found I had lead poisoning I was off work for six months. Then I went back. In three or four weeks I got lead poisoning back again. So eventually, altogether, I was off for eighteen months, with full pay. They found me a job on the weighbridge, and even that started it up again. It was too close to the works, so they put me in another department, away from the works. But, because of the medical results, they were advised to suspend me from work for good. I couldn't get my lead level low enough and keep it down. As soon as I went back it used to go up. So they paid me hardship money. I couldn't criticise the company.

I didn't retire. For a fortnight I worked for Tarmac in the quarry, and then I went to the Mill down Via Gellia, recycling the nylon. When that closed down I was made redundant, so I went back to Friden, where they had a vacancy. That was through asking Walter, because he was still working there – he worked there all his life. And then I were made redundant at Friden's, twelve months later.

Looking back on that part of my life, I have no regrets whatsoever. If I were young, I would do it again. I learnt how to survive on my own two feet. Without work you just wouldn't survive. I was married with a wife and a little child at nineteen years old - I had to have consent from my parents - and I thought, 'I'll make a go of this. That's it.' Leslie was a bit more lucky than I was, but he worked hard in Johnson's Mill down in Darley, just the same, and he worked himself up to be the foreman. You've got to have a chance to show you can do the job. [Louis Vincent]

Wakes week.

Wakes Monday was the big day, after the 24th June. They'd parade at church on the Monday morning, and then they went to the Bowling Green. The Foresters went to the Bowling Green for dinner. After tea they had a parade round the village and there was the Morris Dancers out. The Foresters was a sort of friendly society. There weren't any help in them days, and if any of the men were off sick you used to go to the club and get a certificate and take it to the doctor. The doctor signed it, and they could take it back to the club and perhaps get ten shillings or a pound a week. Well, there wasn't anything else. Twice a year, they used to parade down the street. After the First World War they paraded on Armistice Day, then whatever day of the week 11th November was. [Dolly Brassington]

Wakes and Carnival.

They always called it 'Wakes', and it was ever such a big do. You used to have to save up from one Wakes to another to save any pennies. There used to be donkeys and that at the top of Winster Bank. Timmy Wray used to come every year, and they used to have these lamps that hung down and a flame used to shoot up. There wasn't a mantle over. They used to have these teeth, like, and you used to throw these wooden balls at them. And they always used to have donkeys at the top of Winster Bank. They'd only go so far, and you couldn't make them go any further, yet they'd only trained them for about half-an-hour. The fair people always came from Youlgreave to Winster. After they'd finished the Wakes at Youlgreave on the Sunday, they'd be packed up Saturday night. Sunday morning they'd travel from Youlgreave with the steam engine pulling all these big caravans, swings and dobby horses. It used to be on the triangle up by the Miners' Standard. They only used Oddo Field for the Carnival. Wakes was at the top, but they had Carnival in the daytime, as they do now. Carnival would perhaps start off at 1.30 p.m. and parade up the Street, and they finished off in Oddo Field. Wakes were there all week at the Bank Top. Every night you could hear Wakes going, all over Winster. This would have been anything after 1909. A lot of us lads used to go down towards Dudwood to meet the Wakes coming, and then we used to follow it up. It was something out of the ordinary in those days, because there weren't any televisions. You used to save all the pennies that you could from one Wakes to another. There were always coconuts at Wakes, and that was the only time of the year you could afford a coconut, if you knocked one off or if somebody knocked you one off. There was some who were very good at knocking them off, and they'd knock two or three off eventually, and perhaps they'd give you one. If you hadn't got the money to buy these balls to throw, they'd say, ''ere, teck one of these.' [Bert Boam]

A baby born at Wakes.

There was always a fair on the triangle at the top of the Bank. Tim Wray used to come and everybody assembled up there, and he was there all week. They had swing-boats, coconuts, big horses, slot machines, guns. Auntie Nancy [Mrs George Gregory] used to tell me that one of the children was born there, and she was involved in the birth of this baby, because they were like nomads these fair people, and one of them was born up there. [Roy Walters]

Carnivals and May Day.

We used to have this Mrs Fletcher who lived up here, Dr James' wife. She used to get up the maypole dancing and all that on May Day. There was a May Day Queen in the Main Street. They used to have a maypole and different things. I can't just remember exactly what there was. There used to be carnivals, but it dropped off. I think it would be the war when the carnival dropped off. Then, of course, they started to organise it again. And then there was a break for a year or two and, of course, they've started again with it. [Betty Dexter]

The Women's Institute and the Carnival.

The Women's Institute revived the Carnival and also ran the first barbecues that we had. They became very popular. We had the first barbecue at the Miners' Standard, and it poured with rain, but they opened the room at the back and everybody went in there. The first Market Fair at the top of the Bank was in 1968. I organised that, and we raised £500, and that was a lot of money in those days. We worked all the winter for it. We had whist drives, we dressed 144 dolls to be sold or won on the hoopla, we had a food stall, a craft stall, a roll-a-penny stall, we'd maypole dancing, we'd a marquee with minerals, we'd a marquee doing teas, we sold eggs, we made marmalade, we sold plants, we'd a second-hand clothes stall… I went to Hartington and got two cheeses, Hartington cheese, for the Market Fair, and the Burton girls cut it all up for us and weighed it out. And we had a wonderful day. [Margaret Tomlinson]

A pig in a sack.

The women were involved in the British Legion, W.I., and, of course, the choirs. They organised the Carnival when it was just one day's big event, not every day of the week. I remember my Dad used to give a pig as a prize, and they used to have to bowl the skittles for this pig. I remember Mrs Greatorex winning it, and my Dad putting it in a sack. And she carried it all the way up the Bank [to Bradley House]. It was a live pig. There was Timmy Wray's fairground, and that was lovely - dobby horses that went up and down, throwing for goldfish in the coconut shy, swing-boats, fancy dress and Carnival Queen. [Dot Fearn]

Ringing the fairground bell.

There were no telly. You'd got to make your own enjoyment all the time. There was a fair used to come to the top of the Bank - Tim Wray, with his two traction engines. He had galloping horses, swing-boats and stalls. And he'd got this –

have you ever seen them? – where you have a hammer and hit and try and ring the bell. I can remember when we were kids on a Saturday night they'd be coming out of the Miners' Standard, some of these men out of the village - they'd had a drop too much drink - trying to hit this thing with hammer. I don't know what year it would be Tim Wray stopped coming. Another gentleman took it on, a Mr Sykes, but he'd only got a little kiddies' roundabout and swing-boats. And after that, they never had any more fairs during Wakes Week. It's not the same. It's, like, all gone away, gradually. In them days there used to be seven or eight floats along Main Street. Well, you're lucky if you get one with a queen on now. [Les Bacon]

Piano playing at Wakes Dance.

I remember it was Winster Wakes Dance, and the pianist had let them down, or fell ill, so they asked the MC, Stanley Boam, if he knew anybody who'd play. So he came and asked me and I said I'd try. I'd never done anything like that before, but it went very good, and they said I was better than the normal pianist. So they said would I play regular, and I did, all during the war years. It was good. My piano's at Gill's now - out of tune - and I've got arthritis. I used to play for functions at the Hall, such as if they were having a party. I played a lot of left hand, a good base hand. I wished I could have brought the piano with me, but there's no room. I used to tell people the words, then there'd be a gap for everybody to sing, and then I'd say the next line. [Dot Fearn]

Maypole.

They used to have a May Day with maypole dancing on the first of May. They used to go round the village with it. I used to dance round the maypole. My mother used to dance maypole when she was a child. Two or three sat on it at the bottom and held it, and everybody had May Day off. [Mildred Witham]

Winster Flower Show.

Winster Flower Show was held in Oddo for years and years and years. The Morris Dancers had a marquee always, there in Oddo, and a beer tent as well. And they all got so canned up they couldn't come out with their singing. [John Millward]

Morris dancing.

In the fifties I was teaching morris dancing. I was training the Winster team. I took over from Jos Noton, the headmaster of Winster School. I trained the morris team, and I had a junior team that I used to take to carnival functions and to the maternity hospital at Wirksworth - give them demonstrations there. Jos Noton said, 'We can't work these dances out. We just don't seem to understand from the book.' He said, 'You're a teacher of dancing. You'll probably understand it better.' So I volunteered to go down. I had them dancing and doing it all. They didn't know how to do the Winster Reel. I put it all right for them. I had them dancing, and I danced with them. They was leaning over the desk panting, and I was still dancing, and I said, 'What's up with you lot? I've just got over

Winster Morris, 1952. Back row: Vin Hodgkinson (left), Stan Marshall, Roy Witham, Ray Tuffin, Ray Marshall, Arnold Greatorex, Ernest Glover. Middle row: Walter Herrington, George Walker (Witch), John Wild (King), George Gregory (Queen), Eric Shimwell (Jester), Ron Haddon. Front row: Alan Greatorex, Alan Webster, Joe 'Pea' Rains (Musician), Michael Spencer, Tommy Gregory.

pneumonia and I've got more wind than you have!' Mind you, they were older than me. We were the first team. Roy Witham was a lad - he was 18 - and I taught him the Fool's Jig. We were the first visiting team to ever dance through the streets of Cambridge. Cambridge Morris used to come up here. In the fifties we also had a ladies' team country dancing and morris. I've got the photographs to prove it. I used to take my car with a loudspeaker on the top, and I used to have a record player inside playing the music. And I used to play all their morris dances, because they were all on records. But Joe Rains used to play the melodeon. We called him 'Joe Pea'. He was a greengrocer at one time. It's J.P. Rains, but we used to call him Joe Pea. I tell you, I used to provide them with my car and the music, and we used to go to Hartington, all over the place, and give bits of demonstrations, country dancing and morris dancing, go round with the collecting boxes. We used to give demonstrations at Darley Institute, Peacock at Rowsley. Then they did mixed country dancing, Morris Dancers in their dress and the girls in their dress. Kathleen used to run the ladies' dancers. I wouldn't interfere with their dancing. I used to more-or-less run the show. She used to fit in with us, but we wouldn't allow the ladies to dance the Winster Morris - and that's what they used to get narked about - because it's a man's dance. [Vin Hodgkinson]

'This is morris dancing.'

My husband was a Morris Dancer. We also did country dancing. Mrs Fletcher organised it all, but a Miss Bell - I don't know where she came from - she used to come and give us lessons. There must have been about sixteen girls in our group of country dancers, I think, and there were quite a lot of boys. They did the Winster Gallop, and it starts with this song:

> This is it and that is it, and this is morris dancing.
> A piper fell and broke his neck, and said it was a chancer.
> You don't know, I don't know what fun we had at Brampton.
> A roasted pig and a cuddled duck and a pudding in a lantern.

[Dolly Brassington]

Morris Dancers' pig's bladder.

I must tell you this. My dad was the Jester who had the pig's bladder. After he'd killed the pig, he'd bring the bladder and put it in a bowl of water and salt it and clean it. And then, when it was time for the morris dancing, he'd get this pig's bladder, and I can see him now with a pipe stem and stick it in the bladder and keep blowing. And, by Jove, he used to go red in the face. I thought his eyes would pop out. And he'd rub it on his knee and have another blow and another rub, until he got it blown up. And, of course, when you gave anyone a slap with it, it didn't hurt, because it was so thin. It never burst, and it was clean, because it had been salted. But they don't have bladders now. [Dot Fearn]

The Girls' Friendly Society.

Mrs Fletcher, the doctor's wife, did a lot for the village. She was always working for the village. She lived in the Manse, organising different things. When the war was on - it must have been the 1914-18 war - we were in the Girls' Friendly Society, and we used to go up into her kitchen and she would have all kinds of things on the table, like apples, plums and different things. And we had to bottle it and do, and she sent it down to Darley Hospital. That was called The Willing Helpers' League. We used to go two evenings a week, and that was when the 1914-18 war was on. One night when we went we were all crying, because we were cutting onions up. We couldn't see, because there were so many onions. And I remember these plums ever so well. Gooseberries - I don't know if she'd have somebody collecting them in the village. A lot of the village people had gardens, and they grew a lot of fruit, so she'd probably beg some, if anybody had too much. I do remember that they went to the Whitworth Hospital at Darley Dale. She also helped to organise concerts and things like that - different plays, Sleeping Beauty. She used to help us to get dressed up. [Dolly Brassington]

Silver Jubilee.

I remember the Silver Jubilee [of Queen Elizabeth, 1977]. All the children were given mugs. Silver Jubilee night there was a big bonfire up near Lunter Rocks. I suppose there were others in view from higher points. I remember going up and coming down, because my auntie slipped and did something to her ankle. Mr

Tug-of-War. The Crown Team in action on Main Street on Wakes Saturday 1965.

Boam's taxi took us to Bakewell the next day to the Bakewell Hospital to have it seen to. [Eileen Crowder]

A den of iniquity.

W.I. and the British Legion. That's about it. Whist drives in the Market Hall. There was a tennis court behind the Manor and Mr Fengel used to charge 2d an hour. I used to hear about the Rendezvous - all these doctors and lawyers from Sheffield bringing other people's wives. It was raided quite a few times. They gambled there. It was called the den of iniquity. It was only outsiders doing it on the quiet. [Dot Fearn]

The Manor.

The Manor before Thorntons came was funny, a bit queer - naughty goings on. It was a peculiar place. It ran as a club, men mainly. I never really knew much about it. I think it was a club, and I think it was men. [Marjorie Stoker]

Skating on Mosey Mere.

Another thing I'd like to remind people about, in my days. Everything's altered, both the seasons and everything, because we used to get that keen a frost. I've seen as many as thirty people playing hockey on Mosey Mere at top of Winster Bank – and I've been one of 'em, an' all! And there's been thirty people playing hockey and that on there. It's been frozen that hard and it's lasted such a long while. And now that's never happened for years. The seasons were different then in wintertime to what they are now, ever such a lot different. My father, when he'd finished at the mine, he went to Birchover quarries, and he was out of work for a length of time - as much as nine weeks - with frost. Couldn't work at the quarry for nine weeks, and you didn't get paid. You had to manage the best way you could, like, because most people in the village kept either a pig or two and fowls, and that's how you lived, through your own produce. [Bert Boam]

Bear baiting.

Mrs Staton told me - that's Lizzie Staton, whose grandma lived at Jasmine Cottage on East Bank - that there used to be bear baiting in Winster. The bear used to be baited at the Shoulder of Mutton on West Bank, but it used to stay in the ale house where her grandma lived. I asked her where they used to keep it and she said it just slept in the back kitchen in front of the fire. It would be really weird having a bear lying in front of your fire. But that's all she told me. She didn't remember anything else about it. [Dot Fearn]

The Pigeon Club.

The Pigeon Club used to meet every Friday and bring their clocks. George Wood was secretary, and used to do all the writing down and putting the little band on the pigeons' legs. And then they used to send them away. I was never in the club, so I can't tell you the details. Lots of people had pigeons in the village. There were pigeon lofts everywhere. It was a big sport. They used to have a pie supper every year. I used to cater for them at the Bowling Green. You can imagine making meat and potato pie for about sixty or seventy. I used to bake them in my dad's big tins and take them to the local bakehouse to bake, and then they'd carry them across the road up the steps to the clubroom. They'd all be seated, and there'd be about four of us serving pie and peas. They always had pea and pie suppers, and the weddings and funerals were always the same - ham and tongue salad. I used to bake everything, though, all the cakes. [Dot Fearn]

The Poor House.

In my day it was called Bank Top Farm, but once it was the Poor House, because I've heard my grandma and grandad talk about it. It were very convenient for what it was used for, because there weren't quite as many people on Poor Laws as what there is today. I've been in Burton's shop when people have come in and they've handed over this piece of paper, and I've seen Mr Burton say to the girls, 'Now go and get this.' And it's been a pass for so much bread and cheese, and they had to make that last till they got to Bakewell to the Poor House or to Ashbourne Poor House. [Gladys Hardy]

A poor woman moves on.

I remember seeing people walking from Ashbourne to Bakewell. I lived on the

Via Gellia, in a pub called the Lilies Inn, with my Mum and Dad at one time, and I used to have to bike to school. I saw this old lady going up Shothouse Hill. She was walking. Her shoes were worn out and her feet were bleeding. She said she'd got to walk to Bakewell. So I said, 'Stand on my bike pedal and I'll push you as far as I can, and you'd better go to my Dad's shop to get some money to get to Bakewell.' And my Dad gave her the money for the bus fare. They'd changed the laws so that you could only stop at the Poor House for one night, and then you had to move on to another one, so people had to travel from Bakewell to Ashbourne. They call the Poor House at Bakewell 'Newholme'. It's the hospital now. [Dot Fearn]

The first buses.

There was no transport, so we used to have to leave for school at half-past-seven and ride down with Mr Thomas Heathcote and his milk cart to Darley Dale Station, get the train and then go to Matlock and walk up. And we'd have to walk home at night. My father was quite concerned about this, so he made his way down to Matlock, to a gentleman there, and he got them to send up a taxi for us for half-past-eight each school day. But other people, who wanted to go down to catch the train and that at Darley Dale or Matlock, kept coming and wanting, could they have a ride? It got so overcrowded my father thought he'd better do something else about this. He came down to see if they could set up a twelve-seater little bus first, and then he arranged for it to fetch us back at quarter-past-four in the afternoon. In between that he arranged for them to come up to Winster and leave Winster at one o'clock to come down Wensley and round Oker for the older people to go shopping to Matlock. The fare to Matlock was 6d. And that's how the bus started running in Winster. [Bessie Thorpe]

The doctor and his wife arrive by car.

When we first came to Winster I don't think people went anywhere by transport. They walked. The bank came to Winster once a week, the doctor was in the village, the shops were in the village. Beyond going for clothes, their hairdressing they could get done in the village. So I suppose about once a year they'd go on a shopping expedition - to Bakewell, mainly, more than Matlock. When we first arrived in the village in 1934 we came by car, which shook everybody rigid, and I think I made the fifth or sixth vehicle in the village. The fish man had one, the Dower House had a car, Mr Greatorex had a car, Desmond had a car, and I had a car. Everybody thought I was a scarlet woman - a car and my nails painted red! [Marjorie Stoker]

Village doctor.

An interesting thing, which you couldn't do today, was with the medicines. My husband looked after Stanton-in-the Peak, Birchover, all those villages that side - not Matlock so much, because there were doctors there. Via Gellia he looked after, and the Hollybush down there, the farm, that way. He visited Stanton-in-the-Peak Mondays and Thursdays - I think something like that - and the patients up there would give him their bottles which were empty of medicine, ointment or whatever. He brought them back here where Eileen [Crowder] was working for us, as far back as that. She would fill the bottles and put them in a little box on the wall outside. And you went and collected it yourself. Now, I ask you, today, leaving medicines lying about! An old man, whose name I can't recall, took them down to the bus, put them on the bus, paid the money, and the conductress or conductor took them off at Stanton-in-the-Peak, where there was somebody waiting. Medicine was delivered to the villages on Mondays and Thursdays. It couldn't happen today. Fancy leaving it sitting in a box on the wall outside! It wasn't locked. You just opened it like a cabinet. It would be unthinkable today. You wouldn't dare to, never mind being allowed to. No, everybody just trusted everybody else. It's like not locking your door. [Marjorie Stoker]

A Firework Night accident.

On bonfire night, 5th November, there were a lad about twelve or thirteen year old - somewhere round about that. And in them days, when it were Firework Night a lot of them kind of lads about that age, they used to get a bit of copper piping and they'd drill a hole in this copper piping and they'd knock one end up, and then drum this little hole in. And they used to make their own powder, and they used to get charcoal, saltpetre and sulphur. Them three makes your powder. So they used to make this powder and put it in, and then get some newspaper and get a stick, so it would just fit nicely in your pipe. And they used to ram it in tight, like, after they'd put the powder in. Then they used to light this little bit of fuse. Oh, and bang! It were colossal. Harry Fengel, he was at the bottom of Woolley's Yard - that house at the bottom of Woolley's Yard used to be a bank, William Deacons Bank, once upon a time. And there were a lot of us lads there at the time. And he lit this what'sit, and it didn't go off. And he got it again to light it and it blew him, I don't know if it were two or three fingers off. Harry Fengel was his name, and he lived down the School Lane at that time of the day, across from Redthorne. It was Woolley's Yard that the accident occurred, where the railings were against the Post Office. [Bert Boam]

Hallowe'en.

We'd go and get a turnip, because most of the farmers had heaps of turnips in them days, different to what it is now. They used to pulp the turnips to feed the cows with. They'd always have big heaps, so you could go to one of them turnip heaps, get a turnip and hollow it out and cut little eye things out of the turnip and stick a candle in and then put it on a stick. Today there's no turnips for anybody to hollow out. [Bert Boam]

Cattle fairs.

They used to have two fairs, one in May and another would be August or September. They used to have these wooden pens, and they had some down Pump Lane and they had sheep in them, and they had some up East Bank and they had pigs in them, and so on. For the cattle, they always used to be in the Main Street. My granny, well, she had, one fair day, a great big dish with fried fish in. And then one of the cows went with horns and caught it somewhere, because they knock about so, and knocked pane right through onto fried fish, right against John Rowland's boot shop. To this day there's still a ring in the wall where they used to tie horses up. [Bert Boam]

Earthquake of 1952.

Going out of the kitchen door there was a yard, a toilet, and then there was this big old wall. My mum was in the kitchen and I was somewhere about here, and there was this terrific crash. I went in the kitchen and I said, 'Oh mum, that wall's come down, I'm sure.' I opened the door very gingerly and had a look, and it was still standing. It turned out it was the earthquake. There was this terrible noise, and I thought it was this wall that had crashed into the yard. You wonder is everything coming down on you. [Betty Dexter]

Marshall's Dance Band.

Winster used to be quite an active village, always something going on, very lively, and my father belonged to the Morris Dancers. He had the Marshall's Dance Band, which went quite a few miles in Derbyshire. When the winter weather was bad they used to take a spade in case they got stuck in the snow. The village hall in Winster was called the Burton Institute, same as it is now, and we used to hold dances and concerts - quite a busy place. Also in the dance band was my brother-in-law's brother, Norman, who used to play the piano for quite a while. And my mother played the violin. She was a very good violinist. Learned from the age of five and used to teach. [Phyllis Taylor]

Pancake races.

Mr Johnson organised pancake races, Amy's dad. He were the instigator of them alright, but he always run in races. And they were very good people for giving things away, like. They made cups of tea and gave to folks, 'cause they'd got a big backyard, you see, where all the farm used to be, and they could accommodate up in their front room. [Gladys Hardy]

A Pancake Day accident.

We used to run from the top of the street in those days, down to the Market House. I remember quite a while back when we were all at the top of the street ready to run and Dr Stoker comes down on his bicycle, waving pancake in one hand and riding bike with the other. And he'd arranged with the landlord at the Crown, which was Bert Hawley, to have about eight half pints of beer waiting for us. We set off running down there, straight into the Crown, drunk these half pints of beer and then went down to the Market House where the winning tape was. I got down there first, because I'm a pretty good runner. They carried on with these races for quite a while, but the old organisers were dying off and the new lot taking over, and they only run half the length of the street. I got on to them many a time and told them, I said, 'It's no race, no race at all, running from Woolley's Yard down there, because if you drop your pancake on a short

run you could pick it up and catch up with the winners. I've been on to them many a time. Every year I keep telling them, 'Go farther back', but they won't.

About three years ago I decided to run on my own, at 82 years of age, and I went from the bottom of Woolley's Yard just to show them and prove that you can run if you want. I ran as good as I could do, like, and, of course, everybody cheered and clapped me. Then I used to have Eric Shimwell, who's dead and gone now, he used to egg me on to run. He kept saying, 'Go on, you can beat them.' He used to come and give me a rub down - pretend like - just before the race, and I set off, and I could usually beat them all at my own age, no trouble.

Three years ago there was me and Alun Thomas, because I'd been asking for runners - anybody over 70. But nobody would take me on. Alun Thomas was about 70 at the time, and he said he would do. We set off from Woolley's Yard. I'm keeping up

Picking up pancakes. The Shrove Tuesday races outside the Crown on Main Street, c. 1960, with Carolyn Boam and David Bacon still running.

with him and I'm just about to overtake him, and I don't know whether I caught my foot in a hole or whether it was a cat's-eye, but I went a right purler. I didn't fall, I slid - hands first. Pan went flying, took middle out of my left hand, knocked my knuckle on my right hand…. It was bleeding and they brought me in the house to clean me up. And I kept feeling a bit dizzy. I kept putting my head between my knees. Eric Shimwell was with me. He went straight into Burton's. 'Come quick, Bill's collapsed!' When I came round all I could see was a pair of knees, and it was Dawn Woolley. She'd been in the Police Force and she knew a bit about First Aid. I went to Calow Hospital, and they cleaned me up, stitched my hand up, and I was alright. I've run once since, and I was on my own that time. I said, 'Now then,' to the starter who was the schoolmaster - his name was Edwards, I think. I said to him 'If Eric Shimwell's up there, this is for him, because he's always been on to me.' I just run down for Eric, and that's the last time I've run in Pancake Races. [Bill Slaney]

Youth entertainment.

The Burton Institute was in use most nights when I was a girl. Every week there was something going off. There was always a dance on Saturday night - ball-room dancing and old-time. Vinny Hodgkinson used to run the dancing. It was quite a little hot-spot in those days. We also had the youth club, which was very useful because it had us in contact with all sorts of other villages - Birchover, Youlgreave, Elton, Bakewell, and some of them over Hartington way. We would go and integrate with them. We had sports matches and all sorts of things like that, so we got to know people in the other villages as well as in our own. There was Mrs Fletcher, who used to do the country dancing classes, with Mrs Potter playing the piano. Then there was the Women's Institute, of course. That was very strong. And each church used to have its own concert, perhaps twice a year. The church always put one on on New Year's Eve - that was a good one. [Eileen Crowder]

The Women's Institute.

The Women's Institute was formed in 1918. I wasn't around then, but I know Winster had a lovely ladies choir, which was quite successful. I wouldn't join it when I first came to Winster. I said, 'No, that's for old ladies'. But I did eventually join. They had a Miss Beresford, I think it was, that used to come round from head office in Derby teaching us how to sing, and we won cups and went singing at various events. The first Winster Drama Group was formed in 1949 by the Women's Institute. There were all sorts of productions, and one of them was 'Fall for the Shore'. We were the first amateur dramatic group to do that. We did about six plays in the Burton Institute, and then we stopped and didn't do any more. We had loads of fun. One time we'd about fourteen children, the women, between us, so we got the children who were off school and they helped us fix up the stage. We had to paper it and make all the scenery. And we got Hedley to cook chips for us at dinnertime, specially for us all. We had great fun. It was a big let-down when it was all over, because we so much enjoyed it. [Margaret Tomlinson]

Divorce.

In the 1930s divorce was hardly heard of, and, if it was, it was very hushed up. I know my mother telling me with bated breath once somebody had got di-vorced and I mustn't say anything about it. It was quite a thing. [Marjorie Stoker]

Council houses.

It was brought to the attention of the Parish Council that we needed houses in the village. There was no intention of building them originally on the playing fields. There was plenty of ground otherwise to build houses on. At the top of the Bank, which later they had swings up there, they were going to make that into a little estate up there and then build further out and extend the village that way. But there was one gentleman, whose name was Bill Slack, and for some reason - I don't know why, except that he had no children at all – he wanted houses where the recreation ground was. He thought that would be the best place. He belonged to the Parish Council, I believe, and he got a petition up and took it round to the people who were definitely desperate for houses, because after the war a lot of the young people got married. They came from the war and got married, so we were very short of houses. And he took a paper round to say which do you want, houses or a playing field? And, really, that wasn't the option at all. It should have been the playing field where it was and the houses somewhere else. But, of course, they had this petition and they all signed it, a lot of people, to say they wanted houses. And he worded it so it looked as though they wanted houses on the playing field. So the Parish Council said they couldn't do anything about it. [Amy Slater]

A night out in Matlock.

We use go out every Sat'day naight, go t'dances. Went dairn Matlock Bath one naight, an ah dunno what, ah think i'must've... I fell dairn on flooer. Two girls wer picking maa up when ah cum roun'. Tayen me inter tea room an gi'me a cup o' coffee. I felt not very well all naight after that. Ah went work next day'n dairn farming an doin', an ah wer alraight. Not always bin quiet in mey younger days. Ah've cum in an' stepped out in me best clothes and gon straight back work, never had no bed at all, like, on Sat'day naights. [Stan Heathcote]

The Bull's Head.

Grandmother was owner of the Bull's Head [now Peace Haven, East Bank]. They used to come on their horses, go under the arch, tie them up and go in the pub for half a pint of beer and a packet of Woodbines for tuppence ha'penny. I heard my grandma saying about that. We were always told, when we kept the Bowling Green, that you could never refuse anybody bread and cheese. I don't know whether it was a law. There was a clubroom for functions upstairs, like the one we had. The club was the Buffaloes. It was very private, like the Masons. They didn't divulge, but I know my husband was in it, and they were very good when anybody needed help. [Dot Fearn]

Pubs in 1961.

When I came in 1961 there were just two pubs down in the village, The Crown and The Bowling Green, plus the Miners' Standard up the top of the Bank. Then they made the Hall into a pub, after the factory. It was a factory during the War. It was the Ukrainians. Then it was companion sets, the factory where they assembled companion sets. Then Derek and Pauline Wood did bed and breakfast and obtained a licence to turn it into a pub. [Roy Walters]

The Crown [now The Lodge, Main Street].

The old Crown was going then, across the road, when Will Stone and them were there, but it's been shut about this last thirty years. We used to all go and have a pint. I were only a young lad, you know. I'm sure we weren't old enough. We were only about thirteen or fourteen, drinking beer like a man, and all these old men they didna bother about you. You could sup all night, drink there all night, and at turning-out time they come out and they never wobbled or nothing. They walked straight home, then come next night and have a fill up. They'd tell you some old-fashioned tales, them old men. They shut. It wasn't because it didn't pay - you couldn't get in. It were that full, because old Will was such a comic, and Tommy Todd was usher. He lived at the back, sort of a little flat at the back. He was a sergeant major in the army, and he could throw men out like flies, he could. I've seen many a fight in there. Tommy Todd, he's dead now and gone, he's in churchyard now. I mowed his grave other day. It used to be a real good, old village, an active village. [John Millward]

Minding horses outside the Crown.

Yes, such a lot worked down the mine at that time, but there were so many different trades, same as in a lot of villages. It didn't matter what village it were, there were always someone either to do with pushbikes or some kind of a trade. In Winster there was every trade that you could mention. There weren't any trade missing. There was even a tailor at Winster. People used to come into the village from round about, into same as Winster. I can remember when I were young, some of the farmers that lived away, same as at Pikehall, or someone maybe from Gratton, they would come into Winster for their groceries, saddlers, or something like that. And they would call at Crown for a drink, and they would give you a ha'penny to look after the horse for them. And you thought you were well away then. Sometimes they'd say, 'I'll only be half an hour,' and sometimes they'd be two hours. And you'd be stood there with the horse for two hours for a ha'penny! That happened such a lot of times. I can remember ever such a lot of times that I stood with horse against Crown in the Main Street at Winster, and yet today they're all cars. When I'm talking about there weren't one stood in the street. There was only four in the village. Walter Thorpe, he were first one to ever have a car in Winster, brother to the Thorpe that kept the shop as Yates. [Bert Boam]

Billiards at the Crown.

My Uncle Bill Stone used to keep the Crown. He married my dad's sister. That was when I was going to school. That was his living there, that and pig killing. He didn't do anything else only them two things - look after pub and pig killing. In Crown Yard it were rather funny. You could go up the side and then there were stables there for the horses, because in them days there used to be a lot of horses. Sometimes people would go to the Crown and leave a horse for some reason in stables there. Just beyond the stables was another house. Dennis Wild, they used to live there. It was a nice pub. They had a billiard table and there were a clock, and they used to charge you so much for a half hour, and you had to wait your turn or book. Some days they'd happen be booked up, so they'd put your name down for the next day. So you'd go and have half an hour, because there were no other means of playing billiards. There were no snooker then - it was all billiards. On the footpath today - it must still be there - is two big iron doors, and they opened like a trap door. Horse and dray used to bring these 'ere barrels of beer, and they got 'em on to floor and they used to slide them down there into the cellar on two long pieces of wood. [Bert Boam]

Sing-songs and cyclists.

It was a lively spot in Winster at the time - sing-song every Saturday and Sunday night. At Carnival time you couldn't move in there. Mr Stone used to walk round, 'Mind yer backs, please'. Tray would be over his head, because he couldn't get through that crowd, and they'd be sat outside on the forms drinking. That was on Carnival Day. Christmas time in the Crown you used to have mulled ale - he'd give it away at Christmas - and mince pies. All those have gone now, and we miss all that lot. At weekends they had a lot of cyclists, and there were cycles all up our yard and in the entry up the yard. There were a lot of pots to be washed, and that was my courting, having to wash and dry these pots while the wife was playing the piano! I think that's where they made a little bit of money, because they couldn't make much out of beer in them days. It were only a penny a pint. They used to do a lot of catering. Some came from Sheffield and stopped over the weekend. We'd bed them down up in the attic somewhere. They used to get a lot of beer before they went back. [Bill Slaney]

Piano sessions at the Bowling Green.

I used to play in the pub when they had sing-songs every Saturday night at the Bowling Green, and everybody had their party piece, their favourite song. At Christmas time there was the carols. [Dot Fearn]

Catering at the Bowling Green.

I catered for every wedding round about, because there was nobody else in them days. When they were hatched, matched and dispatched they came to me. The funerals were brisket beef, pickles and that sort of stuff. As for the Friendly Societies, the Buffaloes didn't have many functions. They met in secret, something like the Masons. We kept the Buffaloes' insignias up in the clubroom. They had mayoral collars. They must have had lots of money, because they were very heavy, beautifully crafted things. The Foresters were more like a Sick Club that you paid into. You paid 1d or 2d, and if you were ill you got a little bit, not much. [Dot Fearn]

A ghost at the Bowling Green.

We'd been there quite a while, in the Bowling Green, and Mr Nutt lived next door. He came in one night and we said, 'Tom, have you ever heard about the ghost being here, because I saw this figure of a man going towards Gill's cot.' And he says, 'I'll tell you what he looked like before you tell me!' But I told him it was an old man with one of these Burberry macs, and it was pinned up and he'd got a cap on. And, of course, I said, 'Clear off'. And Tom said, 'That's exactly what I saw.' I had some men lodging with me and one was called Tommy Smythe. He was a Londoner, and he said, 'There's something funny up your stairs. I've seen this old man. He came in the bedroom. I shouted and he went out. I put this chair under the door handle, but it didn't stop him. He came straight through the door.' Then there was Roy Nutt, and he saw him outside in the urinal. I had a gentleman lodge with me who used to come to Enthoven's three or four times a year, and he said, 'There's something happened. My door was going to and fro, and then, just as if somebody sat on my bed, it went down.' But he didn't see anything. But there's no end of people seen it, and I saw it twice. Now, Mrs Britland, who went there after us, she had things go missing and moving about, and she said sometimes the dog's hair would stand up and it would be tense. And David Bentley, who's there now, his wife saw it, and they had things move. He was doing some writing one day in the lounge, and he went up to finish it off, and it was in the next room under something. I asked my Auntie Sarah - she's sort of a spiritualist woman - and I said, 'Who do you think it'll be?' She said, 'I think it will be somebody who never did anybody any harm.' Well, David Bentley's wife, she was in bed, and they'd just got in and she said she saw it, as I did, as plain as plain, going towards Gill's bed. And then, another time, I was going up for some matches and it was on the landing. I just said 'Clear off!'

There's another ghost in Winster Hall. A man jumped off the top. They call it 'Lovers' Leap'. They say he haunts the Hall. [Dot Fearn]

A good head at the Miners' Standard.

Major Evans was landlord in the 1960s and it was sometimes claimed that he gave short measure. Roland Marshall was in there one day and he ordered a pint of beer. When it came there was a good two inches of froth at the top. Roland said, 'Do you think this would stand a whisky, Major?' (meaning would there be enough room for a whisky chaser). The Major said, 'I'm sure it would.' To which Roland replied, 'Then fill the bugger with beer!' [Dot Fearn]

A dispute over football.

One Sunday lunchtime at the Miners' Standard a carload of ex-miners – getting on a bit – came in. And there was an old fellow in - one of locals - called Frank Brothwell. He were in his seventies. And they got talking about old times at Shirland. Now, Frank played football a lot – in fact, he once played for Shirland. And at finish it got into a little bit of an argument, because they said that nobody in Winster could play football, and Frank got a bit angry about it. So he said, 'Well, there's five of us 'ere.' That were four old chaps and Mary Greatorex. And they said, 'We've got a ball int' car.' So they went on back out there, and they played five-a-side. I tell you, there were no Stanley Matthews there, but there were some clog! And Winster won. And they all shook hands, all covered in mud. [Jack Walker]

A tea party.

When I were courtin' missus - name of Bessie Greatorex - one Christmas time I'd come up to see her, and she said, 'Donald – that was her old man – he hasn't come home yet.' It were 4 o'clock in the afternoon. Well, they never served after time in them days. So I went to the Crown to see if they were there, and somebody said, 'They're up at the Miners' Standard.' So I came up here and they were all sat down, and Donald said to me, 'Hey, Jack, come in. Have a drink!' And they had a teapot and cups all round. I said, 'I've not come up here to drink bloody tea!' But it turned out the teapot were full of spirits! I came up to take Donald home, and he finished up taking me home! [Jack Walker]

Winster Hall becomes a pub.

The house we were living in, someone wanted to buy off us at the time, and we had to look for somewhere. We were wanting to live in Winster, so we went down on Carnival day, and all hell was let loose there. There was a fairground on the car park. We looked through the windows and said, 'This is for us, if the rest of the place is alright.' So we ended up buying it. We bought it for £9,750, just before inflation hit. Within three years they told us it was worth £50,000. We sold the Paddock for £10,000. I started to do afternoon teas first, and then bed and breakfast for about three years. I started doing evening meals, and the customers provided their own wine. So I decided that we'd apply for a diners' licence, and then went to my solicitor and said, 'How much would it cost to apply?' He said, 'Not a lot.' So I said, 'Well, while we're doing, how much will it cost to apply for a full-on licence?' He said, 'You can apply. It won't cost you any more, but you'll never get one.' We got the first one in twenty-five years to be granted to private premises! They granted it us at Ashbourne in about 1984, I think. I can tell you a funny little story about that. The solicitor was taking me to Ashbourne. He'd lost his driving licence, and he said, 'I'm afraid you'll have to drive me there.' He'd lost his licence through drinking, and he was applying for a licence for me! So I had to take the solicitor to court to get the licence! I came home all elated. That's how it came about. It went in the paper to say we'd been granted the first licence, and then I got a phone call to say, 'Excuse me, but you haven't got permission for 'change of use' for a pub yet.' It took me two years to get them to agree to what we wanted. They would only allow us one drinking area at first. We'd got parking for twenty-one cars, and so our drinking area was limited at first, and we had to play softly, softly for a couple of years. Then we got it extended and went on from there.

The Hall was a bit like a large family, and there were some real characters among the customers. Some of the older characters of the village became part of the furniture - they were there when you opened and they were there when you closed. They were their own community. We used to have a lady called Dot Fearn. She used to come and play the piano for us. Dot was a good pianist, all played by ear, no music involved. We used to have regular sing-songs, and Boxing Day was a thing to look forward to. Eve Nutt was another customer. Lunch time on Boxing Day was purely musical. People used to sit there and drink and sing, well inebriated, like, till two o'clock in the afternoon. Ladies featured quite well. They had their own community, if you care to call it that. [Pauline Wood]

Winster Hall changes hands as a pub.

It was illness, really, that made us move on. I just became, as I thought, intolerable with my customers, and it's not a very good relationship when you're running a public house. We still get appreciation from our customers. Even now, every time you meet them, they say, 'Why the hell did you sell Winster Hall?' But it's part and parcel of Winster's history, we think. We sold it on as an ongoing business to a gentleman named Mr Warboys. He came from Codnor, and I think he was in Winster round about twelve months. He was an entertainer, which went down very well in the short-term. He used to sing. After a while when he picked the microphone up we used to say, 'Oh, God, it's him again!' He had his old favourite songs. They sounded alright the first time, but when you've heard them fifty times... After him it went to a gentleman, he was an ex-naval man, merchant navy. He must have been there for about two years. I believe he was called Burrows. He tried to run the business like he ran the ship, and, unfortunately, he didn't go too well. He took the bed and breakfast away and turned it into a restaurant, for which there was no real call. Once he'd

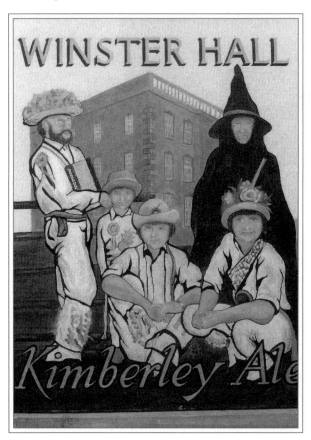

lost his bedrooms, he'd lost the continuity of strangers coming in. He solely relied on the pub and the restaurant, and there was a lot of competition in the area, so that was the death of Winster Hall. He over-stretched himself. [Derek Wood] [Winster Hall is now a private house.]

Winster Hall pub sign.

The sign depicted the Morris Dancers. It was taken from a Morris Dancers' photograph, so the people are real people. The only one I can remember is young Richard Corfield as a young boy. I think he's a grown man now in his forties. [Pauline Wood]

Former Winster Hall pub sign, now on display in the Bowling Green.

Baking and cooking.

Most of the baking was done, because they didn't buy. Same as currant bread, my mother used to make that, the white bread and bun loaf. I remember she used to make a nice fruit cake. She used to bake pastry, meat and potato pie, something with a crust on the top, all those kinds of things. There was cooking done every day. She didn't make bread or cake on a Sunday, but we always had a good Sunday dinner. On Sunday she never cooked anything apart from the dinner. She just cooked the Sunday joint. My grandfather told my uncle off for cleaning his shoes on Sunday. He took them to church and he'd one shoe dirty and one shoe clean. [Dolly Brassington]

What milk and cheese were like in the old days.

Express Dairies at Youlgreave used to have most of the milk from all around here, and milk lorries used to pick them up in churns and take it to Rowsley, but it wasn't pasteurised. But now, with it being pasteurised, they take certain vitamins out of the milk, and your milk can't go sour. It can go bad and it can go rotten and it smells terrible, but it can't go sour. My wife, who was as good a cook as anybody, sometimes she'd say, 'I'll let this milk go sour and I'll make some sour-milk scones.' They were beautiful. But today it can't go sour.

Now, it's just the same with your cheese. There was a cheese factory at Grange Mill, where that furniture place is now, and there was a cheese factory at Gratton, and Chandlers used to have it at Gratton. We used to buy a 30lb cheese, and you used to cut a lump out, like that. And we were not the only people, because big families used to do that, because they used to have great big cheese dishes then. And you used to put that lump on the dish and put the other away in your larder to keep. Where you'd cut out, eventually, if it was left long enough, there'd be little maggots come, and they were beautiful! The older people, same as dad, that's just what they used to go for. They used to cut that out and put it into frying pan and it used to melt just like butter, and they'd dip their bread in. And you'd never had anything more tasty - all the maggots - because it hadn't gone bad. It takes a bit of understanding. It was the goodness that was in the cheese. Today it can't happen because they won't allow any cheese people to make cheese without it's been pasteurised. Nowadays, with it being pasteurised, that can't happen, and so it doesn't matter how much cheese you've got or how long you keep

'there'd be little maggots come'

it, it can't go maggoty. It will go mildewed, but it won't go maggoty. Us lads, we didn't fancy these little maggots, like, but other people, same as my dad, that's what they used to go for. [Bert Boam]

Home-grown fruit and vegetables.

For breakfast we had an egg, bacon. Everybody used to have a pig or a few fowls in the garden. We had a varied diet and a nice roast on a Sunday - big lumps of beef, pork, and anything. There was no shortage of any food, only during the wartime. You grew your own vegetables and fruit - blackcurrant bushes, raspberry bushes, apple trees, everything. We hadn't got a plum tree, so I had to have gooseberries instead. We used to get the milk straight from the cows. And we had what was called 'beesting custards'. When a cow had calved they used to get rich, thick milk, and you used to put it in a pastry, like an egg custard. It was white, very nice. [Mavis Corker]

Broth and hasty pudding.

I think we were very healthy children. For breakfast my mother made us porridge. We had Quaker Oats and sometimes what they call 'hasty pudding'. It was made with flour. You whipped it up with milk until it were thick, and then we had milk and sugar on it. We used to come home from school for lunch and my mother made all sorts for us - broth and roasted potatoes, fried cheese, all sorts of concoctions. To make broth, she got some good meaty bones and stewed them till all meat fell off the bone, took bones out and put vegetables in them. We had what my mother called 'corn beef pie' every Monday for us tea. Of course, she put onion to it, cooled the potatoes and onion together, and then diced the corn beef and put it in later on. Then there was cheese. We cooked it on a plate under grill, and then she spread it on. We had meat at weekend - a rabbit, chicken. My dad used to help to man Wigley's farm, and many a time he'd give him a rabbit, and it were my job to skin it. When we came back from school we had our tea - bread and jam, bread and lemon curd, treacle - anything that was going. My mother used to say, 'Well, you've had a good dinner. That should do you.' At suppertime we had a biscuit and a glass of milk, because we lived near to the milk people. [Gladys Hardy]

Suet puddings.

The women in the village were mostly housewives, and they had to do every-thing themselves then. There weren't any washing machines. They had to do their dolly pegging and the ironing and everything. There was always such a lot of work. And there was always cooking, always. My mother, she was head cook at Hurt's at Darley Bridge, that great big house there - it's a nursing home now, Ivonbrook. Well, my mother was head cook there, and she was ever such a good cook. And we used to have all these steam puddings and everything. You used to have whatever you could catch for breakfast in them days. Same as when the war was on, when you were on ration, you used to have anything - bread and lard or bread and treacle. Sometimes you'd have your big meal when your father come from work at five o'clock. It all depended on the family and where they worked and everything like that. At that time, even the meat was always delivered to your door on a Saturday. You had to have a larder. They used to call it a 'meat safe'. It were, like, ever such fine pinhole netting things on front, and you'd keep that in a cool place.

Puddings was always beautiful, marvellous. Actually, you can't describe to anybody how lovely they were. There were date roly-polys – they were beautiful. The dates in the grocers shop then, they used to be in blocks on the counter, and they used to cut you half a pound off - something like that - and they were lovely them dates were, beautiful. Now you can't get anything like that. Such a lot of things like that, all gone and never come back no more. Marvellous steam puddings. And there's not many people living today, I don't think, that can say they've had mushroom puddings. They used to be lovely. My mother used to make this suety pastry - because you never got any meat but what you'd got a great big lump of suet give you. For every lump of meat the butcher brought you, he'd bring you a lump of suet. And with that suet parents used to make these suety puddings. To make a mushroom pudding you made your suety pastry and you lined a basin. And then you put your mushrooms in, and then put your suety pastry on top of the basin and covered it over and steamed it. All the taste from out of field mushrooms and all the gravy and everything, it were marvellous! You couldn't tell anybody how nice they were! At that time, every season that passed by, there were always loads and loads of mushrooms. There was one period when me and my sister went to a field – and it was not so big, only about an acre and a half – at the top of Shothouse, and we went twice in day with a clothes basket - and clothes baskets in them days used to be rather big, and cane, not plastic. Twice we went in day and got mushrooms. They used to be in circles, like that. Then we sent 'em by Stephen Rains when he were taking his meat on the Saturday morning to the market. And Stephen would take a clothes basket full of mushroom and sell 'em on the market for us. All them days 'ave gone, and they'll never come back no more. [Bert Boam]

'You only waste a whistle.'

When my mother made oatcakes she put an oven shelf from one hob to the other over the top of the fire and she made oatcakes on that - like a griddle - and they were beautiful. She could cook anything or everything - a hot meal, bread, cakes, or anything. For breakfast, you started with porridge, then you went on to bacon, oatcakes, eggs, tomatoes - anything that was going. When we lived on the farm I had sandwiches for my lunch, but otherwise I came home from school for my dinner and went back again. Dinners were whatever my mother wanted to give me - perhaps a boiled egg or something - and then I had a hot meal at teatime with my father and whoever - maybe a stew with dumplings in and all the vegetables you could think of, or meat and potato pie.

I remember some things you don't have now. Mother used to give me sugar on bread, then butter with sugar on. If I'd got a cold and a bad chest, my mother would roll butter in sugar and give it me to eat, and that was very nice because it was real butter, and I think it did my chest good. Then there was beestings. That was when a cow had calved, and it was so many days before it was pure milk. It's what the calf fed on, but it made lovely custard. Grated nutmeg on top and it was lovely.

During the war you had to dig for victory. My father dug a neighbour's garden as well, because the neighbour couldn't do it. He also rented a field with a building, and he had calves and a cow, a pig and fowls. He had the field up here at the top of Woolley's Yard, and he also had a field below the school. We ate very well during the war. My mother made butter, and, of course, when we killed a pig we got all the goodies from that - pork pies and everything. You don't waste much from a pig. They always say, 'You only waste a whistle.' You rendered the fat down, and that was your lard. Bowls of lard my mother had from a pig, lovely lard, smashing. She made pork pies, sausage, savoury duck. She made everything she could. We didn't waste anything. Then we had the bacon and the hams. The ham was beautiful. It was my father that attended to it, and it was him that fed the cow and whatever he'd got, so you didn't get attached to them that much. When we had the fowls near home, at the top of Woolley's Yard here, I got a bit attached to them. My mother didn't feed them. She wouldn't go near them, because she couldn't eat them if she'd fed them. Providing she'd not fed them, she could eat a chicken or anything. We were well fed. [Mildred Witham]

Domestic arrangements at the pork butcher's.

On one side of the range there was a little boiler for making hot water, and sometimes it was used for cooking. I've seen a lot of people drop in tins of peas or beans, anything in a tin that just wanted warming, to save putting them in a pan. If the water was very hot and the boiler was full, you used to tie a piece of string round your tin, so that, when it had been in long enough and you thought it was warm enough, you'd haul it up with the string, so as not to burn your hands. With practice, over the years, you got used to the range. Say your fire grate was full, you knew very well then that your oven was going to be very hot. If you wanted to stew something, or simmer it very slowly, you would let your fire down so that it wouldn't be so hot.

If the little boiler that you had on the range wasn't big enough to hold enough water, say, for a bath, you had to get it really hot so that you could add some cold water and make enough to have a bath. We had a copper in the corner that we could heat water in. My mum also used it for making brawn, boiling pigs' heads and skinning all the skin after they had cooked for about two or three hours. She used to put them in bowls with a plate and weights over the top, and let the brawn set, and it was lovely for cutting, beautiful!

You weren't able to do any sort of fancy cooking on the range in the kitchen, but you could bake pastries and cakes - what we'd call good, old-fashioned, plain cooking. My favourite treat for breakfast as a child would be fried bread with syrup on. It was lovely. Another exotic treat was Brimstone Treacle. It was to cure your cough, and I think it was a kind of sulphur and black treacle mixed up. We always had a good dinner, because there was always loads of pork and sausages. We always had good meals - we were very lucky that way. During the war food was rationed. You were glad of anything. A lot of people wouldn't normally buy offal, liver, kidneys, that sort of thing, but during the war years they were very pleased of it. Spare ribs or anything they were glad of. No, it was very bad for people, especially the big families. We'd ration books.

Many people kept their own animals, but they had to register them. You were getting over your allocation. My dad fed and bred pigs, and if he could push one on the side, not register it, he'd get a bit extra. But they were supposed to be registered. So the person who had a pig in the back yard had to register that. We used to say, 'Have you got any black market meat?' That meant, had you four pigs or six? And if your sow had six and you only registered four, you got away with it. They called it 'black market meat'. [Dot Fearn]

Slaughtering pigs.

That was across the road from Vernon House, up the gennel [now gated] next to the house [Roselea]. Newtons live there now. There was Joe, Dolly and Connie - three children. We used to go and play there, and in their back yard was the slaughterhouse. We used to go creeping in and watch them kill the pigs and watch all the blood running out. A gruesome thing! I wouldn't do it today! It was part of village life. But they were scrupulously clean. Yes, and the swilling and that. You would smell disinfectants and things like that, chloride of lime, which in those days we used to use a lot of. Jeyes' Fluid, I don't know if they used Jeyes' Fluid in the butchers', but there was an awful lot used. The butchers' shops - all wood, of course, which there wouldn't be now - they were scrubbed meticulously clean each day, and always these cloths to wipe things with. [Marion Drinkall]

Pigs and bacon.

Vernon House, that's where Joan Wild lived, and these little buildings at the back used to be them sort of buildings, like a pig cote. We called them pig cotes or pig houses, I don't know. Such a lot of people used to have these places for keeping pigs, because I should say there must be half of the people had pigs in them days, because that's what you lived on - rabbits and your own free-range eggs, kill a pig and have your bacon and your hams, and so on. Just going upstairs we'd always got hams and sides of bacon hung up. This is how you used to live.

At Winster, you know the Bowling Green. Now there's two bungalows built up there against the Headlands fields. There used to be six pig cotes. In the gritstone there was a chute, so you'd no need to go inside to your pig. You could just stand there and tip your slop and that down into the trough below, down this chute. There used to be a lot of competition, because you could rent them off of the council. One person would go in for Saddlebacks and somebody else would go in for Large Whites, and so on. And a lot of people out of the village used to go and have a look to see whose was doing the best.

My Uncle Bill Stone, who kept the Crown at Winster, keeping the pub and pig-killing was his living. There was another pig-killer and his name was Sam Heathcote. He'd kill for people at Wensley or Elton. Nearly every day that come in Winster you'd hear somebody having pigs killed - always squealing. On your way to school you used to go and ask for the pig's bladder and blow that up and you had that for a football. They used to kill them just in the back yard. And the blood - that was beautiful! You had to keep stirring it so it didn't congeal, and you put salt in, and that's how you made your black pudding. My wife used to make beautiful black pudding. The fat that was in was lovely out of the pig, whereas the fat today would poison you, nearly, when you taste it. I can remember when the war was on we used to have bread and lard, and it was lovely, because it was proper lard out of the pig. My wife used to make all our own sausage. We used to get sausage skin, and I'd have to put them into salt and water for twenty-four hours. And then you had to scrape them all to clean all the sausage skin, and then you put them on your sausage machine, put your pork in and turn the handle, and it keeps filling, and you just give them a twist - and that's how you used to make your own. You put so many onions in, so much bread in, and so on, to make your sausage - pork, onion and bread - and they used to put sage and thyme in. And it used to make it ever so lovely. Your own brawn, which is, like, pig's head, and everything like that in brawn and jelly, it used to be a smashing taste.

When the Second World War was on, and you did some black-marketing, there was a chap from Bakewell who used to pay £1 a pound, and he'd fetch these hams. And we used to go to the hairdressers in Bakewell, and they used to go into the back, and he used to weigh them there. That was when I was living up Arter Hill in Bonsall. My wife's mother lived in the first house. And, just a yard or two from the house, there was a coalhouse. So when you were killing a pig you had to swill the coal dust away and get a table and face your pig down, and you had to be careful it didn't squeal, because you weren't suppose to kill them - it was the black market. We got this pig, and I asked Hilda to hold him, and then you'd hit him with a hammer to stun him. Well, silly beggar, I didn't hit hard enough, and I didn't stun him enough. So we grabbed hold of it and on to the table, and I was in that big a hurry, frightened of it coming round, I got the carving knife, and I shot it in and it come right out the other side. Somebody in the village might have reported it, if they'd heard the pig squeal. [Bert Boam]

Vernon House.

Well, first of all, I remember Vernon House as a very happy home. We used to have a big garden at the back and a stable with the coal in and logs, and during the war a pig, which we kept half for the Ministry and half for ourselves. Over the top of the steps there you would go into the loft, where I used to play as a child. Round the back was, like, a pigsty, which we didn't use in those days. On the other side there was the place we used to do the laundry and the washing and that. Before that, it was a dairy with a cheese press and two coppers, but I believe now it's part of the cottage next door, which, of course, has been sold off. Above that, Norman used to have his joiner's shop, where I used to go and watch him making lots of different bits of things - furniture - and really enjoyed my time up there, playing with the shavings when I was much smaller. There were beautiful steps on the outside. Of course, when I went to Vernon House later they were all down - no joiner's shop, none of the garden with the beautiful well in, which was all dressed stone and it had a rope on. One day I turned the handle and the rope went to the bottom. On top my father used to have lots of fossils, all on top of the well, and there was a beautiful path all the way round. There was a wall that we used to sit on, a flat-top wall, then flowers, then a garden at the top. At the other side was, like, a grotto, which was all lovely. My mother used to empty the dolly tubs and swill all that on the yards on a Monday. It was very large and it was always kept that you could eat your food off the floor. She would chuck buckets of water and brush it with the brooms, oh yes, to get the water down the grate and keep it clean.

In the inside we had a living room and a little utility room, and then there was the back door. On the other side there was the sitting room and then the pantry and the scullery. Under the stairs was a wine cupboard, which is now a toilet, I think. Fair enough, that was a good improvement, but it was the opening up of the sitting room into the pantry and scullery-kitchen that upset me, because it was completely out of character. It really upset me, that. [Marion Drinkall]

Setting up home.

We rented a cottage before we were married. It had been empty for years, and it was just a two-up-and-two-down, and all the walls inside were whitewashed - either whitewashed or bluewashed. And underneath that was a layer of what they called 'red raddle' - that's what Granny Roper called it. There'd been re-pairs to the roof, which was quite good, but the rest of the house was very, very damp, and I made it worse, because I had the hosepipe on it to try and soften this lime to get it off - well, a stirrup pump, that's what I used, because we had these stirrup pumps handy in case of incendiary bombs. I made it very wet and I scraped and scraped and scraped this lime off, then bunged all the holes up, but it took us a long time to get it habitable.

We had this house for some months before we married, then I lived with Granny Roper for about a couple of months until we got the furniture, which we had to buy second-hand, because there was no new furniture, except that utility stuff. We had utility chairs, I think. Granddad Roper took us to a second-hand shop in Bakewell and he bought a lot of furniture for us - bedroom suite and things like that - which I didn't value at the time, but I wished I'd kept it. There was an old black range in the kitchen with a hole in the bottom, and another black range in the sitting room, a bigger one. The house belonged to Sammy Rains. His grandfather had left it him. So I went up to Sammy and said, 'Look, I want the drains done.' I'd got Jane outside in the pram, and there was a rat running round on the garden, and I nearly had a fit, because I don't think I'd ever seen a rat before. I said, 'We want some new drains and I want some new fireplaces and things'. I think we paid him about ten bob a week rent -

eight shillings, that was it. Anyway, he wasn't forthcoming, so we put the new drains in ourself. [Margaret Tomlinson]

Bert's two grannies.

Them steps go up to that little cottage [Greenlees Cottage] at the side of the Post Office. My granddad and grandma lived there. She was blind, my granny were. Her name were Granny Boam, and when we lived at Post Office my Granny Boam lived there at this little place. Next to the Hall [Glendare] was my Granny Holmes, and she had a fish and chip shop. My brother's wife lives there to this day, only it's been altered. There was door off the footpath, and you went down a long hall. Well, that's been made up now. My dad bought a bit of ground belonging to the Hall, so you go into a door up this jitty at the side now. Where the door was on the front it's made up now. To this day, there is a cellar. When my granny had it you could go up the hall and open the door at the top and go down some steps and you went into the cellar. And when you got down into cellar there was a big gritstone - they call them salt-stones - for salting pigs. When you'd killed your pigs you'd salt your bacon on these salt-stones. Then right in the centre there was a well, and it was always full of water. It's still there to this day, but it's covered over now. In the back yard there's a pigsty, and you used to keep your pigs there. When my granny lived there you had to take your pig through the house. [Bert Boam]

Gentle chastisement.

My father was Horace Johnson and my mother, before she was married, was called Nellie Swindell. I was brought up in a very loving home. My mum was the one that always had to chastise us - but we knew that she loved us - because my dad never wanted to chastise us. I can remember my brother and I were once falling out about the rice pudding skin, and my mum said, 'Horace, speak to these children.' And he gave us the least little tap and it didn't hurt at all, but we cried just because my dad had done it. We were brought up in a very loving home. [Amy Slater]

Rich and poor.

My father was on the Parish Council, and sometimes they would have the meetings in his house, and it was suggested that they give the old people five shillings at Christmas. Now five shillings would be twenty-five pence now, but it meant more in those days, and, of course, Mr Thornton [then Chairman of the Parish Council], with having all the money, said 'Well, I think it's neither here nor there. I don't think the old people would really appreciate that.' I remember my father said, 'My word, some of those people would be really pleased at that.' [Amy Slater]

Recent history of Winster Hall.

Mrs Marsland lived there, I think, earlier this century, and she lived there alone. I don't know anything after that until Mr Widdison. He ended up to be painter and decorator with his two brothers, and apparently his mother ran a guest house there. 'Putty' Gregory, who used to own the petrol pumps, apparently bought the Hall simply to sell the lead on the roof, because he bought it quite cheaply. But the Peak Park stepped in and made him put the lead back, and it was more expensive, so it wasn't a very good deal in the end. I think it then passed to the Army - displaced persons and things like that. It had a bit of a motley history then. There was a factory there, where they made the companion sets and toasting forks and things, and that was run by Mr Bennett. I think it got knocked about then, but the front two ground floor rooms stayed as they were. They must have used them as offices, a front for the business.

I think the panelling was there during the Hall's time as a factory. Then Keith and Pauline Witham bought it. He was a builder and turned it into four flats. He sold the panelling off to an antique dealer, because the dealer came to my front door and asked me if he could measure the lounge. He'd apparently got these pieces all stacked up in a room and someone wanted to buy it. And he wanted to know how it fitted together again, so he'd come to see where it originally was to get an idea how to put it back together again. It remained as flats until we changed it. We started doing bed and breakfast first. We changed the bedrooms into letting bedrooms, with two flats on the top floor - one for our son and one for us. [Pauline Wood]

Washday.

My earliest memories would be of mother - she'd be fetching the clothes in, so it must have been a Monday evening - and sitting on her knee on the settee. Something felt cold, and I looked down and she'd got a slug on her leg, and I was frightened. Yes, that was the earliest one. [Marion Drinkall]

A child drowns in a dolly tub.

I was born in 1909 in the bedroom over the top of the Post Office at Winster. I had three sisters and three brothers. Winnie, the eldest, used to live on Winster Street at Kirby House. While she was there she lost a little lad who was about two to three years old. She was washing at the sink and he was playing about with the dolly tub and dolly pegs. He dropped a peg over into the dolly tub - there was only about seven inches of water in. He said, 'Splash, Mam.' She said, 'Yes,' and carried on at sink. He tippled over whilst she was at the sink and broke his neck there and then. She grabbed him and run to Dr Fletcher at the Green Gates - the big house that is up for sale now - but it was too late. It would have been in the 1930s, or perhaps before, because it was when I worked at Mill Close Mine. I'd been playing with him because I was on shifts two till ten, and it was about twelve-thirty I was playing with him. And when I came off at ten o'clock I found this is what had happened. [Bert Boam]

The same drowning tragedy.

Little Eric Spencer's death was a real tragedy. His mum was washing in the kitchen with the dolly tubs. Eric was playing around. She spotted his little red jumper in the dolly tub, and she said. 'Oh Eric, why've you thrown your jumper in the water?' Pulled it out and, of course, there's a child drowned. She ran to Dr John Fletcher at the Dower House. He came running, but it was too late. He couldn't do anything. Terrible. Eric's sister was my friend. I can remember. So sad. [Dot Fearn]

A child's death at Great Close.

I've never, and I don't think any human being has ever, been as frightened as I was once there. It's a wonder I didn't die, I can't understand why I'm here really, because I was that frightened! Joe Heathcote, the name was. He had four cows, and he used to bring milk into Winster from his farm at that time. And there used to be a bit of competition with selling milk, and he used to cart it from Great Close with the yokes and two cans, and it was thre'pence a quart. And he had twins, and one of them was taken very bad with convulsions, and they were three-and-a-half years old. One of them had these convulsions and they had to get Dr Fletcher to go (he'd something the matter with one leg, and he used to go with a limp - Dr Fletcher, the one that lived up the Bank, then, across from the Chapel up West Bank, before Dr Stoker took it over).

But Dr Fletcher didn't want to go to Great Close unless somebody went with him. Joe Heathcote had a lot to do with my mam and dad. We used to have some milk off him. He asked if I would go with the doctor, because it was such a rum road. You had to go through the wood, over the brook, and it was very muddy. I was about ten years old. You had to go, because your parents used to make you go. So I went with Dr Fletcher, and he saw to her, and then I had to go back with him to Winster with a storm lantern. And, when I got back, news came that she'd got bad, so I had to go again with Dr Fletcher, but I hadn't been in the house very long and she died. Well, I'd never seen any child die. I'd never seen anybody dead. And they were all crying and making a wailing noise, because they were spiritualists or something, and it frightened me to death. So I went back with Dr Fletcher for a second time to Winster. And then it come midnight, and they called for me to go up to Great Close again, and he said, you'll have to go and fetch Mrs Critchlow to lay her out. Well, Critchlows lived then where Wigleys live now, the farm right down Painter's Way. I come down wood, and, with the little girl dying, it upset me, and, as you were coming down with the storm lantern and you stood on a rotten piece of wood, it fair made you jump, and I got frightened to death. Then I had to go and find my way across the brook to get to Critchlow's. Well, the brook were roaring, and as I tried to find a place where it was narrow so I could jump, I jumped into the brook - and my light went out! I screamed and I don't know what did happen, I was that frightened. I don't know - you can't tell anybody, because I don't think anybody could have been more frightened than I was then. It was gone midnight, I was alone, and all you could hear was the rush of the water. And the storm lamp, I lost it in the brook. But I did manage to find my way to the farm, and I nearly kicked the door down. 'Oh heck, Mrs Critchlow,' I said, 'come down, quick, like.' When I told her what had happened, I said I was never going back there no more, and I said I daren't go to Winster now. Somebody's got to take me back. So her son, Billy, he brought me back to Winster. [Bert Boam]

Childhood illnesses and death.

There was the cart that came, refuse or whatever it was, emptying the toilets. That was horrible! Oh, we've come a long way from there - the tin bath in the back kitchen, having a bath on the Friday night. You had to have one bath a week, whether you wanted it or not. If you go in Winster churchyard and have a look at some of the gravestones - behind my mother's grave I think there's four – you'll see that loads of children never lived to five. They hadn't got the medicines, the know-how, the antibiotics, like they have today. I know my husband lost his brother with diphtheria, and his mother got it. But, by the time they found out what it was, Stanley had died. Later they were able to treat them. There were children I knew who died. There was two little boys in the village - it was so sad - one was called Eric Stone and I can't remember the name of the other little boy. I know his surname was Hardy, and they were only children. It was doubly hard, because the Hardys never had any more sons. Then there was the Heathcote family, who lived at the bottom of East Bank. There were four of them taken away with this diphtheria. Of course, with these two young children dying, they knew what was wrong with the others, and they got better. They went to an isolation hospital in Bakewell. Quite a few died of measles. I know Mrs Gilding's daughter did. I remember having these measles at the same time as Joyce Gilding, because my mum and Mrs Gilding was in the surgery together to see the doctor, and he told them to wrap them in hot rugs and a mustard bath. 'Put this mustard all over them and wrap them up in this warm cloth.' My mother's aunt was sitting with me at the time, and, when she heard what Dr Fletcher had said, she said, 'You're not doing that to her. We'll keep her warm, but we're not putting any mustard all over her.' I was very ill, but I recovered and Betty didn't. Mrs Gilding covered her in mustard and followed what the doctor had said. When my son was small he had a very, very bad convulsion, and Gill, my daughter, she'd had one. They said put her in a cold bath of water. Well, I did the same when Paul had his, and the doctor said he'd never heard of such a thing. You see, there's nine years' difference. [Dot Fearn]

A tragedy in the Thornton family.

When the Thorntons lived at the place which is now called the Manor, they'd allow several of us girls to go and play on the tennis courts. These were the Thorntons who started the Thornton's toffee company. The little Thornton girl died in the big lily pond. Somehow she just wandered off and was found face down. It was terrible at the time. The whole village was in mourning for that little girl. She'd only be about three, I should think. It was terribly sad, that was. They'd got five more children, Michael, Shirley, Sandra, Penny and Rosemary. [Marion Drinkall]

Laying out the dead.

When people died they used to lay them out in their own house. Fred Wilson used to go with a board and lay people out and measure them up and make the coffin. You booked a coffin and decided the sort of coffin you wanted. You'd say, 'Well, I want to have it so big and made of such-and-such a thing and those sort of handles.' My mother's coffin was solid oak. Now in this day and age you don't have to have these mass-produced things if you get to the right joiner. We used a friend of Roy's. He was a joiner, and he took on his father's undertakering business when his father died. So, when my mother died, Roy got in touch with this friend of his, and he said, 'Yes, I've got some seasoned oak in my father's stock.' My mother's in the graveyard, and her mother and father are next to. [Mildred Witham]

'I've saved it for when the time comes.'

The first one was my granddad, Charlie Braithwaite. He lived at Woolley's Yard, and he'd not been very well. So auntie said, 'Will you go and put the blackouts up to the window?' So I did that and lit the lamp. I said, 'Are you alright, Granddad?' He said, 'No.' And I said, 'No, you're not alright', and turned him over, and I could see that he was dead. So I shouted my auntie up, and she was upset, of course. And she said, 'Let's put him in this white shroud. I've saved it for when the time comes.' So I helped to lay him out, and she says, 'Aren't you upset or bothered?' I said I wasn't frightened of my granddad. And then it happened again, with a lady who lived nearby. She died in her armchair, so my husband and I carried her upstairs. And she'd got a best lace nightie, which I put on her, and she looked very nice. And then there was Mr Wild, who lived next door to me, Harold Wild. He died one Friday dinnertime. His wife thought he was choking, but he was dying. So, again, the same ritual - his best white shirt. And we laid him out in it, and he looked very nice. [Dot Fearn]

The 'New Look' after World War II. Eva Heathcote (left), Mildred Witham and Freda Heathcote outside Mosley's shop in Main Street.

Teenagers, a house-proud mum, and grandma.

When we were teenagers we used to go to Matlock. There'd be quite a few of us. My friends were Marjorie and Evelyn Boam, Hedley's sisters. They were really nice girls as friends, and they were at school with me. We were always together. If I wasn't down there, they were up here at my mum's. Oh yes, we were great friends. We still are. My mum was clean, spotlessly clean, but she didn't make our lives a misery. She was a bit houseproud. If you'd gone in and been smoking and dropped your cigarette ash, she'd come out with a brush and pan. She used to say, 'It's a bit of a beggar - you're here bringing your friends and me mother's stuck in there on her own'. [Betty Dexter]

Self-made music.

They didn't have television then. More people used to play the piano and sing. I went down the road to learn the piano from Mrs Dale. She lived down at Newlyn on West Bank. [Betty Dexter]

Courtship.

Girls used to get together, and we used to go on the monkey-run. All the girls and boys used to meet on Winster Lanes. They used to walk backwards and forwards, you know, pick one or pick up another boy. Well, I met Stanley Marshall, and we just sort of clicked, and that was it. I'd known him for about four years. We married 9th September 1939. [Annie Marshall]

'Can I carry your milk can?'

The Reverend Ware married us. I wanted a church wedding, and I got married on a Thursday, because I didn't want a lot of people there. It was a cold day, but it was very nice. David, my husband, came from Eagle Tor, Birchover. The first time I ever saw him, he was getting the milk from my uncle's farm, Frank Roper, at the top of the Bank. I used to go up and take the dog for the milk at night, and this young man was stood outside the Miners' Standard with a friend. As I went down what we call 'the Hollow' with the milk to get on to the West Bank, I heard these footsteps come running after me. He'd whistled before, but I never turned round to a whistle. He just came to me and he said, 'Can I carry your milk can?' It all started like that. He walked as far as Marshall's shop with me, and I had to go a few yards further down, and he just said, 'When can I see you again?' So I said, 'Well, in a couple of days' time it will be my birthday. Come and play the piano for me.' [Marion Drinkall]

Dancing and courting.

I was quite lucky as a young girl, as there were a lot of men around in the village to dally with. Vin Hodgkinson used to hold this dance session in the Burton Institute every Monday night. It was the highlight of our week. He'd got a radiogram, all Victor Sylvester's records. If you couldn't dance, Vinny would teach you, because he was professional. If you could dance, all well and good, you went round. There were loads of partners with the soldiers being here. It was

6d, and it went on from seven until eleven, so we had good money's worth. I could do everything. I liked the Maxina and the Military Two-Step. I liked a nice Waltz and Quick-Step. It was at this time that I met Roy. That was a one-off, but he was very nice. He was very posh, and I went down for a holiday, but it never really got off the ground. It wasn't 'Mr Right'. When I met 'Mr Right' we were at the Lilies [a pub on the road to Cromford], and I wasn't very old, but he was nice looking, and, you know, when you're about fifteen, sixteen, you start to look round. I thought, 'He's nice.' Anyway, he went in the Army, in the Desert Rats. He volunteered and he was abroad for, what, six years - a bit more, I think. The night I met him it was Youlgreave's Well Dressings, and I was playing in a dance band, and who should come in but Richard - you know, the one I fancied a bit. He came in and he waited for the dance finishing, and, when I went outside to get in the car, he appeared, and he wanted to take me out the following night. And that was it. [Dot Fearn]

Married and called up for the army.

I got married in 1939 and came to live at Winster. The place where I first went living was a little cottage in between the Crown [now The Lodge] and the Post Office. I'd been married three weeks when war broke out, so naturally I had to go into the army. I spent four-and-a-half years in the army. When I came out and back to this little cottage, in those days there was no water laid on. The toilet was outside, and, with the wife's parents living at the Crown, we used to use their toilet instead of going outside, which was a water toilet in the Crown. We had to fetch water from standpipes. There was one down Pump Lane and one up Woolley's Yard, and those were the two nearest. A few years later they put water in every house. There was no electric in Winster when I was courting, only gas. I think it was just before the war when electricity came to Winster. So those were the amenities that we got soon after I got back. [Bill Slaney]

First television.

Roy only came to Winster [1961] because we had a television! There weren't many televisions about. Dad had a cabinet model with a nine-inch screen and a magnifier on, and we used to have the room in there full for Cup Final days, with all people from round about that wanted to come and have a look, because we were one of the first to have these televisions. [Anne Walters]

Clipstone comes home.

Grandfather Adams had two horses, Clipstone and Toby, and he kept them in the stables at Hillcrest on the Flat. I think they've now been made into the front room of the house [Chimney Cottage]. Unknown to grandma he sold Clipstone to the Wakes people, Tim Wray's. Of course, by the time she found out it was too late to get him back, because the fair people had moved on. But twelve months afterwards she was making bread on the table in front of the window, and, when she lifted her head up, there was Clipstone looking through the window. She put him in the stable and locked him in. And when grandfather came

Above: 'Roping-in' at the wedding of Betty Brandon and Ernest Dexter, Winster Primitive Methodist Chapel, East Bank, 1967.

Below: 'Roping-in.' The rope is untied when the bride and groom pay up.

home that night she made him go up to the fair people and give them the money back. That was exactly twelve months afterwards. So Clipstone came home for ever. [Betty Dexter]

Gyp the dog.

Our little chummy, our Gyp, was a little terrier, and he used to run out every morning. He'd meet Miss Buxton at a certain place as she went on with the letters all round the banks and that, and he'd be back on our doorstep ready for Annie Stone and myself. He'd take us down to school, see us safely to the schoolyard, and he'd toddle back. He'd be there at twelve o'clock, and he'd take us back, and he'd be there at four o'clock. This little dog, he'd always be on the trot ready to meet us. Aye, deary me.

Well, it was election time – and I could tell you a few tales about elections in Winster. In the Main Street the Liberals had Vernon House (Mr John Wild's) as their committee rooms. So one morning little Gyp was toddling up from school, and they got hold of him and took him in and dressed him all up in these yellow ribbons tied all round him. Of course, little Gyp goes toddling up the Main Street, and further up there was Mrs Ellis' Conservative committee rooms. Of course, they got hold of the little dog and all the yellow ribbons were thrown away. There he came decked all up in blue and took us back home. That's something that has always lived in my mind. [Bessie Thorpe]

Times were hard.

We used to go into shops in those days and say, 'Put me in the ledger book.' They used to call it 'putting on strap'. Then they'd pay at the weekend if they could - probably pay what they could and let a bit go over to the following week. There was a bank in the village and also a Post Office where they could put money in. We had these little metal boxes where you used to put all your bits of soap in, and then, when you were washing up, you'd shake it and get quite a lather on. In retrospect, everything wasn't pleasant. I remember things like having to sit in the dark to save money or because you didn't have any candles or whatever. We used to sit with the firelight to save putting a penny in the gas meter or light a candle. People had to save, and it was always instilled in you that you mustn't spend all your money. Put some on one side for a rainy day, which I'm afraid they don't do today. They enjoy themselves while they can. [Dot Fearn]

INDEX